MIXED DOUBLES TENNIS

Clark & Carole Graebner
with Kim Prince

MIXED DOUBLES TENNIS

McGraw-Hill Book Company
New York   St. Louis   San Francisco
Düsseldorf   London   Sydney   Toronto

This Book was set in Century X by University Graphics, Inc.

123456789BPBP79876543

Library of Congress Cataloging in Publication Data

Graebner, Clark, Date
Mixed doubles tennis.

1. Tennis—Doubles. I. Graebner, Carole, joint author.
II. Title.
GV1002.8.G72   796.34′228   72-10043
ISBN 0-07-023879-0

Contents

Poteris modo velis
(You can if you will)

MIXED DOUBLES TENNIS

INTRODUCTION

The Life
of Riley

In the early days of tennis, the sport was a game for the rich and soft—a privileged pastime shared by the gentle folk of a select country-club fraternity. Those who played seemed larger than life—international luminaries, ambassadors, and the original great sportsmen, such as René Lacoste. The courts of lush and slate-smooth grass or perfectly swept *en tout cas* were lined by marble tables and lawn umbrellas. The play was pursued in a genteel fashion. Nearby was the hum of soft conversation and the tinkling of iced drinks in crystal goblets, proffered on silver trays. The afternoon shadows seemed to give the players an almost delicate hue. The world saw the sport in this regal setting as a lingering, enchanting interlude.

Our world of tennis has been quite different, both in its beginning stages and now that we're part of the fastest-growing sport in America. It's been no less enjoyable for either of us, however, because tennis is the same thrilling, captivating game now as in those more idyllic days. We have played all over the world, in every possible setting, as representatives of our country, as individual competitors, and as professional athletes pursuing a vocation. The game itself is a unique attraction, still very much the lingering, enchanting interlude; only the setting and characters have changed. Tennis is a recreation, a sport, competition at its best, and for us it has been a way of life. In the day of the jumbo jet and indoor courts, tennis is a sport for all seasons. All people—young, old, male, female—want to play.

Because we've grown up with tennis and been part of the sports transition from pastime to life style, we have some very definite ideas on how best to play and enjoy the game. Needless to say, as so-called "experts" or "pros," we can instruct you in the mechanics of better play. We can also impart a special philosophy and flair for tennis that have made it so much a way of life for us. But make no mistake concerning the aesthetics of the game. To play it well, using superb shot-making, complex maneuvers, and cunning tactics, takes hard work, dedication, and concentration. Those attributes have taken us to Wimbledon and Forest Hills, Australia and Southeast Asia. We don't expect those feats from you, however, nor do we feel that is the only way to realize the full pleasure of the game. The recreational and friendly competitive levels of a less frenetic approach are equally pleasurable. We still play regularly on that level. The game is enjoyable no matter what your proficiency. Believe us, in many respects the friendly game is as much fun as being on center court at Forest Hills in front of a stadium crowd of 10,000 and a national TV audience!

We've been called from time to time the "perfect" mixed doubles team. That's a bit extreme. Our tournament play has been extensively covered by press and TV, and since we're married to each other we usually know where we can find a partner for a match. The "perfect" ends there. Circumstances have contrived to provide the rest of the reputation. For that we're grateful, but take no special credit.

Individually, we both are lucky enough to have been nationally ranked in the top ten, and as a pair we have had an exciting and rewarding time, both on and off the court. Each has been present for the other's great victories (and some not-so-great defeats), and our mixed doubles has always been a refreshing respite from the pressures and strain of singles competition. Our "famous tennis pair" tag is one we're proud of. We'll tell you how it began, how we've fared, and how we suggest you approach your own mixed doubles. It is the game for a lifetime.

4

CHAPTER 1

Where It All Began and How We've Done

CLARK: *In early summer of 1960, I had just returned from the Wimbledon junior championships; I was happy (having won the tournament), eager for more success, and about to meet my future wife, Carole Caldwell. Louisville was the first stop on the summer junior circuit for both boys and girls. Billie Jean King (then Moffit) and Carole rode into town from California about the same time I returned from the perils of foreign conquest. My recollection of that week is quite simple: we met, played tennis (not together; at seventeen you don't practice with girls), ate cheeseburgers (together), and vowed to meet on the east coast later in the summer. As a member of the Junior Davis Cup team, my first stop in the east was the South Orange Championships. Carole was there, and we made a date for the Saturday-night tournament dance. When I discovered that the college all-star football game was on TV Saturday night, it turned out that my tie was hopelessly stained and my cuff links had mysteriously disappeared. Carole didn't buy any of it, but dropped the dance idea anyway, happy, I assume, to let me go my own way. In those easy, friendly summer days, our lives progressed without much thought about the future, but the die had been cast. The following sum-*

mer after a year at Northwestern, we met again in the east. Marty Riessen, my friend and doubles partner, had a Ford Thunderbird that served as our transportation from tournament to tournament. Often Carole and her friend, Janie Albert, would travel with us. We were one big happy family as we made our way from Merion to Orange, Longwood, and Forest Hills. The four of us were inseparable; Carole and I, even more so. By the next summer, my tennis was improving by leaps and bounds, my knee needed an operation, and Carole had become an integral part of my life. While recuperating from knee surgery in the fall, I decided Carole was the woman for me. We became engaged the next spring—April of 1964. After debating on a wedding date for several weeks, we decided on the following December. We promptly moved it up to September and then again to June. Our parents were confused, our fellow players were laughing, the news media were eager for a story, and we were oblivious to it all. Our reasoning was obvious: We thought it would be most fun to play that summer as a married couple. We were married on our return from Wimbledon, four years after our first meeting. The ground work was now set for the "famous tennis pair."

In those four years of developing courtship, we had made literally hundreds of friends in the tennis world. We began to appreciate the growth potential of tennis. Small but avid crowds were auguring well for the future. Possibilities for development were being explored by large civic-minded groups, commercial concerns, and private foundations. The sport was expanding all around us, as we were beginning to realize our potential as players. Tennis was coming of *age and luckily we were in the right place at the right time. Naturally, in subsequent years we have developed additional alliances and pursuits, but our friends and connections in the tennis world are indispensable to us.*

That summer and until I turned pro with the advent of "open" tournaments, our life was almost carefree. We were doing what we loved; our needs were in great part provided for, and our responsibilities were few. The accusations and counter-accusations of professionalism and under-the-table payoffs for amateurs were still a faint rumbling in the distance. We were all to be affected by it later, but for the time being the spirited competition and the support of a new wife seemed blissfully pure and rewarding. "Those lazy hazy days of summer" were indeed very good to us.

In point of fact, Carole's reputation and ranking in 1964 were far loftier than mine. She was ranked in the top ten, and I was tabbed as a "comer." We were both twenty, but Carole had realized her potential at an earlier age, as many girls do. In those days the amount of expense money we received (per diem) depended on ranking and current tournament performances. Needless to say, my per diem was a paltry sum. Hot dogs for me and filet mignon for the star of the family! By the third or fourth round of tournaments, I was usually gone, but Carole was invariably a semifinalist or finalist. Not much for the ego, but a fact I simply had to face, and resolve to do my best in matching my new bride's brilliant performances. It was to be three more years before I fully realized my potential, however. Had I considered that prospect, I might well have thrown in the towel right then, but a big victory always seemed just around the corner. This brings up one of the greatest assets of being married to another player. We had each other as cheerleaders and morale boosters. At one stage that first year, I remember confiding to Carole my doubts and anxiety over improvement and achieving a better record. Grad school, law, and business all presented possible alternatives, and when I lost they seemed to be infinitely preferable. I was sorely vexed by the whole situation. (Carole was prepared to give up the tennis circuit as well, which was a lot to ask of an established front runner.) To her everlasting credit she was not only philosophical about that prospect but instrumental in buoying my spirits and confidence in my own game. Happily I did improve (slowly), she continued to win, and the "game for a lifetime" was still with us.

Carole was having her finest year, winning one title after another. At Forest Hills she reached the finals. After losing in the third round, I began to feel like a side show. But in one respect I was grudgingly benefiting from this experience: the family standard of excellence was being established, and the star was regularly assuring me that my day would come. Occasionally, cheering for each other, we found ourselves in peculiar situations. In the quarter finals of Forest Hills that year, Carole was to play one of her oldest and toughest opponents, Karen Susman. Their matches were always tooth-and-nail affairs; there seemed to be no love lost between the two. In contrast, Karen's husband Rod is a fine fellow and we had become good friends. In this particular setting, we assumed our positions in the respective corners of our wives, fully prepared to cajole, inspire, and coach each to victory.

The girls hotly pursued their skirmish, fighting for every point in a close match. In loyal husbandly fashion, Rod and I said nothing, but ended up laughing convulsively as our wives went at each other in maniacal fashion. Afterward Carole and Karen went their separate ways (Carole had won) and the two coaches adjourned to the locker room for a friendly beer. Carole and Karen joined us later and for once we all had a laugh. Although it's not always easy to fall in step with a tough opponent right after a match, the camaraderie of fighting the same good fight is a lasting one.

We often compare notes on opponents. In planning strategy for big matches, it's easy to miss an opponent's weakness that might provide an opening at a crucial time. Having the other to assess those strengths and weaknesses can be an ace in the hole that carries the day. I'll often ask Carole her opinion on plans of attack or whether she's noticed any flaw peculiar to my opponent I ought to exploit. Her help has sometimes meant victory instead of defeat for me.

All but the most experienced tennis fans are awed by the ability of ranking women players to hit the ball with men. Carole dazzled everyone with her strong game, and she'd take particular relish in smoking the ball by the male opposition. Her expression seemed to say, "The bigger they are, the harder they fall." The fans loved it, and Carole just grinned. One year in Egypt we won the mixed doubles title and the novice fans were incredulous at Carole's play. They shrieked, waved, laughed, and applauded, as we blitzed the field with Carole belting the fuzz off every ball she could get to.

For several years, Carole and I lived almost exclusively in the limelight. From week to week the venue changed but the competition, and growing success for us, continued. We traveled all over the world, savored our victories, and shared our private moments together as tennis nomads. We couldn't help feeling ours was a unique life. However, there are those sobering moments in the tennis world when one begins to feel like a man without a home, or even a country. At such times, the companionship of a wife experiencing the same dilemma is invaluable. The other married players were either phoning wives nightly or footing the expense to bring them along as pure luxury. Carole and I were grinding the same ax, at the same time, and it was all dutch treat. We were playing the game we loved, meeting new people, and we were together all the time—unprecedented good fortune for tennis players.

CAROLE: *Seventeen was a great age for me. As a member of the Southern California intersectional team, I was traveling the summer circuit and exploring the new world of a budding tennis star.*

I'd come a long way from the fears of my first day on a tennis court in Santa Monica, California. As is so often the case, my initial failing (the kids made fun of my inability to hit the ball) drove me to greater effort and zealous pursuit of excellence. Years of hitting against a garage door, late-night practice sessions with my grandfather, and begging the older kids to play with me were bearing fruit. The mocking laugh had long since faded away.

Our team, including Billie Jean Moffit, had traveled

to *Louisville for an early-summer tournament. I remember well being happy and eager for victory, but
have no recollection of my first meeting with Clark.
I've been told by Dave Reed, a fellow California player,
that we met the first day of the tournament. As hard
as I've tried, I cannot recollect that first cosmic event.
So much for love at first sight! Obviously the fellow
was not in best form that day. Later in the week a
friend informed me that* the *Clark Graebner, former
Boy's Champ of the United States and recent Wimbledon Junior Champ, wanted a date with me. I'd never
heard of him. He couldn't be that special. My friend's
description brought no recollection of our initial meeting nor did it inspire me further. The date failed to
materialize. My coy reaction: Let the lad show his
face in person, then we'll talk.*

*Later in the week after having both lost our semi-
final matches (I to Kathy Chabot and he to Frank
Froehling), we met for real. I had heard by now of his
"superboy" (later to be "superman") reputation for a
rather impressive physique, but I was appalled at his
seeming arrogance and haughty posture.* Even with
glasses he was not a bad specimen, though—not bad at
all. In any case, he began to pay a great deal of attention to me, and I was being swept off my feet by this
junior champion who fed me cheeseburgers and lemon-
ade. Later that summer at the Eastern Grass Court
Championships in South Orange, we met again with
considerably more excited anticipation. After a broken*

---

* At fourteen, Clark contracted osteochondrosis of the spine, a result of
too rapid growth. He was forced to wear for support a brace which gave
him the appearance of a strutting tin soldier. Even today his posture is a
bit exaggerated—stiff and erect; this impeccable carriage is sometimes
misconstrued as arrogance.

date (the stained tie, missing cuff links routine) I remember telling Billie Jean: "I'll never accept a date from that lug again as long as I live!" Her retort was: "Wouldn't it be funny if you ended up marrying him?" My anger and humiliation were all-encompassing—no likelihood whatsoever of such an insane event! Naturally we did cross paths again. The following year after an overseas tour on which I beat Margaret Court (now Smith), the National Clay Court Championships provided our rendezvous. The ever-present Billie Jean and I were practicing one day, and from the next court came: "Hey, when are you gonna go out with me?" Whirling around I saw that goofy grinning "superboy." My halting retort, "Sorry, forgot my cuff links," fooled no one, and the rest is history. The following months were sublime: four of us in Marty Riessen's T-Bird were discovering tennis at its best. Janie Albert (the famous football player's daughter) was the fourth, and we presented a comical scene, piling in and out of that car at every tournament. We felt like characters in the adventures of Huck Finn. Within this traveling circus, our romance was blooming. Two years later, Clark and I were married in the middle of our tennis escapades. Little had changed in our lives—we were both pursuing more vigorously than ever our "game for a lifetime."

During these years, my game reached its zenith. Luckily for one so young, I developed great confidence, and nothing breeds success like confidence. My enthusiasm for the sport was boundless. Every day was a holiday; every meal a banquet. In the early sixties before the advent of the big professional purse, amateurs had guarantees for expense money, and whether you won or lost was not always critical in immediate financial terms. Due to high ranking, my weekly guarantees were excellent. Most of us were, as yet, unscarred by the more hardened ethic of the professional athlete. In retrospect, I believe we were all somewhat naive regarding our positions as amateurs in a Simon-pure tennis world. But unsavory implications are not always clear when one's life seems so rosy and perfect. The year Clark and I were married, I was ranked third in the United States and sixth in the world. There wasn't a female player in the world I had not or could not beat. If that's not riding the crest of a wave, then tennis balls aren't round. I loved every second of it.

Alas, my husband, the aspiring "superman," the holder of countless junior trophys, the sultan of tennis swat, Clark Graebner, was ranked a lowly twenty-four in the United States. It was a hard row to hoe; that situation would be unsatisfactory for any proud male. But I knew his day would come, as, of course, it has. We'd joke about it, and he'd call himself "Mr. Carole Graebner." The tennis world felt sorry for our predicament, but we never did. Ultimately we had the last laugh: both ranked in the top ten of the world.

Although we have both helped each other over the years with our respective games, strategy, and assessment of opponents, we have at all times maintained and protected in each other individuality on the court. To restrict that individualism would hinder imaginative and inspired play, and that's the key to a champion's success. This mutual understanding let each of us define his own competitive qualities and pursue the victory in his own way. Within that framework, we helped the other as much as possible, but never pushed. Clark was developing his own style at his own speed. When the levels of competition are highest, the progress is slowest; it can be a very discouraging proposition. My success at the age of twenty was not the norm, and Clark was just beginning to see the light at the end of the tunnel. I think I knew long before Clark that he would be a world class player; I saw it in his court presence and competitive drive.

The press was not always that understanding. Sportswriters seemed to take special glee in creating outside pressures on us. No matter what our individual records or achievements, we were always compared, and the implications were not always flattering. Individual accomplishment just didn't seem to be in the sports page vernacular. Only recently has my name not been mentioned in programs, saying that I outranked Clark in the United States for many years. For those who took peculiar pleasure in that discrepancy, I had and have only contempt. The knowing and cynical smiles they wore were only signs of their insensitivity.

Learning to adjust to each other's routines was an easier bridge to cross. I favored a regular routine: breakfast, practice, rest, lunch, match play, et cetera. Initially Clark was rather undisciplined in his regimen. He disliked practice (he's never been a good practice player), and he tended toward extremes in his living style. But over the years he has developed his own routine, and he performs his best when circumstances allow strict adherence to it. Also, sharing the waiting and worrying made it easier and eliminated much of the monotony of the touring player.

I learned early in our marriage that those clean white shirts and perfectly pressed shorts weren't helping my backhand any, but they were a reflection on me as Clark's wife (or so I thought). I made sure he was sartorially splendid by becoming washerwoman supreme. I ironed everything except his socks and stitched the smallest holes with meticulous care. Those labors of love were the envy of the bachelor players who were forever running out of clean whites.

PART OF THE TEAM "RETIRES"

CAROLE: *For several years we continued our tennis odyssey together. There are those who say the tour is tedious, a grind, and generally a worthless life. I suppose there is some truth in that, but those criticisms can be applied to any pursuit at one time or another. When I retired from full-time play, it was for none of those reasons. Winning is stimulating, and never worthless, at least in my experience. To excel in a field and be recognized as one of the best in the world is an experience shared by only a very few. I never tired of it. Perhaps that sounds immodest; if so, I'm guilty of a most satisfying indulgence. Champions seem to be made that way. Pancho Gonzales is the aging lion of tennis at forty-four; he still wins, he still loves the game; and the world loves the man more than ever. We're all birds of a feather—winning is addictive. Very few step off the crest voluntarily. My demise was quite human, and, I guess, predictable —I became pregnant. No misgivings, however, for that event was as exciting to me as any championship. I simply turned my attentions to another challenge: motherhood. The baby, a home (in New York City), and retirement all came within a few months. The change was abrupt, but not, as I had feared, difficult. We have two children now, and they have been sensational additions to our world.*

None of this is to say I've abandoned the tennis world, or vice-versa. Except for rare occasions (Forest Hills and Wimbledon) I no longer compete. But I am now involved in the sport's administrative functions. As captain of the Federation Cup and Wightman Cup teams, I've had plenty of involvement: the development of younger players and the excitement of international competition. It's not time consuming, and yet I'm very much a part. In many respects it's more challenging and interesting than competing. Having one of their own as a leader helps the players, and both teams have done extremely well. I also do promotional work for Bonne Bell cosmetics as beauty, fashion, and tennis consultant, and advertising work for World Tennis *Magazine. My past tennis achievements and connections are invaluable in these areas, and I have the opportunity to stay current with the latest developments in all facets of the tennis world.*

CHAPTER 2

Mixed Doubles

The game of doubles and mixed doubles is quite different from singles. The addition of the two alleys and a partner to join the play demands varied and different strategy. It is a game of control, finesse, and imagination, requiring all the spectacular shots in modern tennis. Position and teamwork are of the utmost importance. How well you and your partner get along, cover the court together, and complement each others' abilities and styles will determine the success or failure of the team. There's no substitute for ability in purely individual athletic endeavor, but in a partnership, compatibility and clear understanding of team objectives can go a long way to blunt the individual brilliance of an opponent. Doubles requires this special expertise. There is nothing as interesting and exciting as two evenly matched doubles teams both storming the net exchanging rapid-fire volleys.

Because of the normal difference in strength of the man and woman in mixed doubles, every rule for regular doubles is even more important for mixed doubles. When even the most brilliant men players have trouble teaming effectively, it's easy to grasp the importance of good teamwork between the opposite sexes. The inherent differences are going to complicate matters somewhat—so accept it and be prepared.

THE AGONY AND THE ECSTASY

Some men absolutely refuse to play mixed doubles. The reasons for such abstinence are as varied as the ego of each man: inferior female ability; lack of competitive zeal among women; poor mobility and weak shots—all more or less chauvinistic judgments. Unless the man is an absolute fanatic or in rigid training for the men's title at Forest Hills, these complaints are generally without substance. It's every bit as challenging and takes just as much ability to carry off good mixed doubles. Nor is a weaker woman partner likely to destroy the balance of the team. A partner who can effectively complement your play is the best bet. If the big game is your style (cannonball serves, crashing overheads, killing volleys), look for a partner who is a steady, dependable player. The ability to keep the ball in play is an absolute necessity if you are to have the opportunity to hit the big shot. By the same token, if you are most at ease retrieving and stroking the ball easily, concentrate on placement and setting up the winning shot. In many cases, the crucial shot is not necessarily the one that ends the point. It's a placement that puts the opposition on the defensive, making it possible for the stronger partner to rush in and put away a weak or defensive return.

If the woman possesses a reasonably strong game, there is no need for a big strong partner. A dependable serve and crisp volleys by each partner are an ideal combination. Balance in your attack seldom fails. There are two of you to cover the court, and an overanxious and careening partner will only confuse the teamwork.

CAROLE: *Before Clark and I were married, we played our mixed doubles in perfect balance, covering the court almost fifty-fifty: he took his shots, I took mine. And we were quite successful, indeed. After our marriage, Clark, in a natural inclination to assume more responsibility, began taking more of the shots. The percentage ratio became more like seventy–thirty. He took most of the overheads and roamed the net like a hungry tiger. This new tactic, however, did not destroy our teamwork, because he is a naturally strong and aggressive player. Our success continued, and I took great pride in being able to set up Clark for the "big kill." (Underneath, I knew the experts and sage doubles strategists were attributing our success to my cunning ability to utilize Clark's best abilities.)*

CLARK: *Carole has excellent ground strokes. Her game is steady, and her return of serve is consistent. I can always depend on her to make a forcing drive which gives me the opportunity to cover the net with abandon. This is my style, and the tactic works because we are capable of complementing each other. Her steadiness sets up my strong net game.*

As you see, there are no hard and fast rules; seventy–thirty may be as effective as fifty–fifty, depending on the abilities and strengths of the partnership.

Of overriding importance is the desirability of finding a partner with whom you get along. It's virtually impossible to play well and enjoy the game if you are dissatisfied with your partner. This is true of any sport. If you're at odds with your teammates, the natural reaction is to blame mistakes and failures on them. In tennis, this leads to a lack of concentration on your own game, and the next thing you know, the team is suffering and your frustration is not only evidenced in poor play but very likely in deteriorating relations with other players. Do yourself a favor: choose someone whose game you know, whose style complements yours, and most of all, someone who is an amenable partner. Then be adaptable and easy going.

CAROLE: *One of the greatest parnters I've had in mixed doubles is Marty Riessen, for one simple reason. He gives his women partners total confidence. Whenever we played together, his encouragement and patience were terrific. "Carole, you've got the shots; just get the ball in play and we'll go from there." That is an excellent mixed doubles philosophy.*

THE GARDEN OF EDEN

(A brief note for male chauvinists and women's libbers)

There can be no battle of the sexes in mixed doubles; you're on hallowed ground now. Enjoy your partner and forget the conflicts, contrasts, and inherent differences of the opposite sex. It's a game and as such should be enjoyed. The competition should bring out the best in both of you.

THE TEN COMMANDMENTS

Our good friend Bill Talbert, a champion doubles player for years, former Davis Cup captain, and famous doubles strategist, has ten time-tested pointers for mixed doubles. We call them, for your benefit, the "Ten Commandments." They are guaranteed to bring the greatest enjoyment to men and women and even to the most hardened critics of mixed doubles. We've used them on and off for years and recommend them for their basic honesty.

Women:
1. Always let your partner appear to be boss (the only concession we'll ask). Someone has to be captain, and even if he isn't a better player than you, chances are he thinks he is. Flatter his ego and be satisfied with letting your racket do the talking for your side of the team.

CAROLE: *As Clark and I were walking onto the court for the mixed doubles finals in one tournament, he turned to me and said out of the blue, "Carole, there are two of us on this team, and only one captain—you are not it." My jaw went slack. I was dumbfounded until I realized it was the first tournament we had played together since our marriage. Such are the labors of love! We won.*

2. Pay attention to what you're doing on the court. It's a tremendous temptation in informal mixed doubles to let your mind wander, gaze idly at the surroundings, or look for the children playing nearby. This is disastrous. If your partner is taking the game seriously, as most men do, he is probably livid at your lackadaisical attitude. Know the score and concentrate. He'll appreciate it and your own game will stay sharp.

3. Allow the man to serve first. Even if his crashing

serves result in excessive double faults, his confidence will be enhanced by your support. Also allow him to play the left court in receiving service. His feeling of importance in playing the "crucial" points on that side may improve his game. You can always give him at least one lead a game, by winning the first point.

4. Never gossip with the other lady across the net. There is nothing quite as distracting to men as partners carrying on a non-stop discussion concerning matters of no relevance to the match. An idle laugh in the middle of a serve or exchanged trivialities of only feminine worth will tax even the most loyal partner. If you must talk, restrict it to praising your partner, and never during the point.

5. Don't be a junior partner. Remember the shots you play are just as important to the team as your partner's. If you're playing fewer than he, more reason to make them count. Make every shot a forceful and intelligent move.

6. Don't wear jewelry. Tennis is not a cocktail party; it's a game of movement and exertion. Bracelets, necklaces, or flashing rings will only decrease your mobility and distract your partner. Hitting an overhead with a jingling, clinking, sparkling mass of feminine fashion next to you can be an almost impossible feat. By the same token, women will find serving while wearing bracelets or rings impractical at best.

7. By all means, show up the other man if you can. Women are often better players than men and mixed doubles provides the perfect opportunity to rub it in. Pass him at net and smilingly ask if the pace is too fast for him. Your partner will love it, and it's a guaranteed crowd pleaser.

8. Don't make effusive apologies for errors. Whether the mistake is critical or not, no amount of wailing and whimpering will correct it. Better to turn your attention and concentration to the next point. A simple "sorry," and an added concentration with subsequent success is the best possible apology.

9. If you and your partner are a new team and unfamiliar with each other's play, always tell him of your weaknesses. He may wish to compensate right at the outset. If your backhand is weak, he'll perhaps want to position you in certain situations for the team's advantage. Don't wait until midway in the match to confess sheepishly an inability to hit overheads when you've both been running madly for the baseline at every lob to your side. Let him in on your secrets, before they become obvious.

10. Above all, play to win. Tennis is a game of competition as well as recreation. Playing mixed doubles is great fun; playing to win is even more fun. There is nothing unladylike about competing for the victory. Winning gracefully is far more rewarding than losing gracefully.

CAROLE: *I hate to lose a point whether it's the first or last one in the match. I'm out on the court for a total effort and I don't like to lose, period. There's nothing unfeminine about that and I've found that most men I've played with have been overjoyed with my determination.*

For Men:
1. While you stand firmly on the baseline, balls in hand, poised to serve, ask your partner if she'd like to serve first. She'll get the message. If there's any hint of a

discussion, nip it in the bud with a: "Well, we'll try it this way for openers."

2. Position yourself in the left or ad court and politely ask your partner if she'd like to play it. You've taken the responsibility of playing the critical "ad-in" or "ad-out" points and so you had better live up to your own billing or be prepared to switch. Sometimes it's better to switch than fight.

3. Don't pick on the opposing lady unless you have to. You'll incur the immediate wrath of the male opponent at this "easy out" tactic. Spare your woman opponent the embarrassment of being made the goat and enhance your own position by winning the points through the opposing man. Be satisfied with winning enough points to gain the match.

4. When you're serving to the opposing woman, always use a slice or spin serve. You avoid the embarrassing tactic of trying to overpower her and yet the slice or spin is just as difficult to return as a cannonball.

5. Always suggest rather than command. Make your partner feel as important as possible. Include her in your thoughts on strategy and ask for her suggestions. She'll doubtless take a greater interest in the match, concentrate more, and generally play better tennis.

6. Don't force your partner to play net if she's incapable of it. This is an extreme measure, but her effectiveness within the team will be blunted if she is unfamiliar with the territory at net. Encourage her, yes, but if she fails, adapt your play to take advantage of her strengths from the baseline. This is purely a mixed doubles compromise.

7. Avoid any comments or actions that tend to denigrate the play of women in general. You risk a grave offense by insinuating the gals can't hack it with the men. Modern-day women tennis players have, as the saying goes, "come a long way, baby!" It's a touchy area and best left completely alone.

8. No matter how great the temptation, choose your partner for skill rather than beauty. Don't forget your conviction that you're in it for the sport and competition. Also, non-playing wives or girlfriends have a tendency to get touchy about these things.

9. Don't contradict your partner's call in mixed doubles. She may not be as sage in the game, but her eyesight may be better. A simple contradiction on a judgment call is often disastrously insulting. There are better ways to counteract a call if it is flagrantly wrong than by contradiction.

10. Give your best: women like winners!

CHAPTER 3

A Refresher on Stroke Production

No doubt you've read or been told many times the correct methods of stroke production. We are assuming that you have at least a partial understanding of the various strokes, and so we won't belabor the issue. But as a reference and refresher, these basics are always helpful (these tips are given from a righthander's point of view. If you're a lefty, simply mirror the directions and apply the same principles to your strokes).

THE GRIP

One of the most difficult aspects of tennis about which to offer advice, without personal knowledge of the player's game, concerns the grip for different strokes. Grips are very much a matter of comfort and personal adjustment. For expediency in modern tennis because the ball is being hit harder and faster than ever, we recommend only two grips: one for the forehand and another for all other strokes.

Forehand Grip For the forehand drive, the "shake hands" grip is the norm. The "V" between the thumb and forefinger is on top of the handle, and the large knuckle of the first finger is on the righthand corner of the handle. The palm is behind the handle and the fingers are spread to give support and solidity.

Backhand Grip This grip is used for the backhand drive and is easily adapted for the serve, overhead, and volley. The hand is moved about a quarter of a turn to the left from the forehand grip. This positions the large knuckle of the first finger on top at the right-hand edge of the handle, and the "V" between the thumb and forefinger on the left hand corner. It is an easy adjustment and not difficult to make during play. For both grips, your whole hand should be on the racket; how far up or down the handle is up to your own "feel." If you find yourself choking up on the grip, chances are the racket is too heavy. The racket is designed and weighted to be held near the end.

THE SERVE

The serve is the money stroke, the most important single shot in tennis. It is the one stroke in which you have complete control. You, not your opponent, manipulate the ball. If your serve is weak or inconsistent, poorly placed or short, it's your own fault. It's also the one shot which you can practice by yourself. Master the serve and you've taken a big step toward being a winning player. Most importantly, the serve is one continuous motion. You should develop a smooth-flowing serving stroke. Essentially the stroke is the same as the ball-throwing motion. Pretend the racket is a ball and throw it toward the service area. It's as easy as that. The first motion you make backward transfers the weight to your back foot. As you swing the racket forward, the weight is transferred to the forward foot. The power in the serve comes, as in throwing the baseball, from getting the racket behind the ear, then stroking out. At no point during the serve should your arm stop moving.

The Service A consistent toss is the key to a good service. The ball should be placed in the "striking" position so that you release it only when your arm is fully extended. As your arm uncocks from behind your ear, the motion is one of throwing the racket head at the ball. At contact you should be leaning into the serve with your body and arm fully extended. Remember, the serve is one continuous motion.

When you step up to the baseline to serve, your body should be sideways to the net, and your feet should be spread from twelve to eighteen inches apart. When you serve to the forehand court, your left toe should be about an inch behind the baseline, and your left heel about six inches behind. In other words, your feet are not parallel to the baseline. The racket should be cradled in the left hand and facing in the direction where you want the ball to go. You should be relaxed and in balance.

A vital part of the serve is the toss òf the ball and point of contact. The object is to place the ball in the air exactly where you want to hit it. The ball should be held in the fingers of the hand, not the palm. The hand starts at the waist as the motion begins and rises slowly, releasing the ball only when the arm is fully extended. The ball should be struck at its highest point, with a full extension of the serving arm. The arm should never be bent at the moment of impact. The toss should be in front of the left foot. If allowed to come down, the ball would land about a foot inside the court. At the point of impact, the body, arm, and racket could be compared to the leaning Tower of Pisa. If you can achieve a good toss, the rest should come easily. Keep in mind that there is no rule in tennis that says you must hit the ball once you toss it. If, by chance, you make a bad toss, stop in mid-swing and start over.

THE FOREHAND

The forehand is the main weapon in most people's game. It is a natural motion, one that comes easily to us. Most of our day-to-day hand actions use a forehand

The Ready Position In the ready position, face the net with your racket held directly in front of you, waist high. Be alert. You should be on the balls of your feet, knees bent, prepared to go either to the left or right.

motion—applauding, waving, hammering, closing doors, et cetera. Because of this familiarity, most people's forehands are stronger than their backhands. From the ready position, knees bent, and in balance on your toes, you should pivot on your right foot, turning your body sideways to the net. As you pivot, the racket is taken straight back, remaining perpendicular to the ground all the way until it points behind you. The motion should be kept compact since too long a windup can result in a late hit. As the ball approaches, your left foot should move forward toward the point of contact and the left shoulder should face the net.

The Forehand The body is turned sideways to the net. The knees are bent as the weight moves forward onto the front or left foot. The racket face is perpendicular to the ground at the moment of impact. The wrist is firm and arm steady and your eye is on the ball all the way to the strings. The ball is met out in front and the stroke continues toward the target point.

The knees remain slightly bent and weight rests mostly on the right foot. Finally, the weight is shifted to the left foot as the racket comes through and makes contact with the ball. The ball should be met well out in front of the left leg as the weight continues to shift during the follow-through until it is almost entirely on the left foot. Your racket moves through and upward, remaining perpendicular to the ground. The stroke should be toward the target area. Try to avoid swinging the racket across your body. Keep the stroke on the same path as you wish the ball to travel. The object is to carry the ball on the strings as long as possible, to provide maximum control.

THE BACKHAND

Though many people have troubles with the backhand, the hazards are more psychological than real, since the stroke is more natural than the forehand but you can't prove that to most players. You are swinging away from your body, not into it. As you pivot to hit a backhand, you should turn the racket slightly to the right in your hand to assume a backhand grip. The shoulders turn to the left as you get your feet into position (sideways to the net), and the racket is swung back, cradled in the left hand. When the backswing is completed, the racket head will point directly away from the net. Both feet should be pointing toward the alley although you have not taken a step, merely pivoted to the left. As you are about to hit the ball, step forward on your right foot and transfer your weight from left to right foot. The knees should be bent as you concentrate on getting down to the ball. The swing itself should be a graceful sweep, contacting the ball well out in front of the right foot. Your arm and racket should form an angle to keep the racket head from dropping below the wrist. The wrist should be kept firm—not laid back, not leading. The backhand is hit with the shoulder, arm, and racket, but not the wrist. At impact the arm should be firm and fully extended. The follow-through is on a slightly elevated plane with the right arm still extended to the target area.

The Backhand The body is turned sideways to the net, the knees are bent as the weight moves forward onto the front or right foot. It is essential to get down to the ball, hitting it at waist height. At the moment of impact remember that the racket is an extension of your arm. The wrist is firm, the arm straight, and the ball is met well out in front. The stroke continues toward the target point on an elevated plane with the arm fully extended.

THE VOLLEY

The volley is probably the most mis-hit shot in tennis. That's because it isn't a stroke as much as a block or punch. Too many players make the mistake of taking a full swing at the ball even though it's moving toward them at great speed from close quarters. This presents a timing problem that makes a good shot nearly impos-

The Volley (Backhand and Forehand) The volley is met well out in front with a punching motion. There should be practically no back-swing and the distance the racket travels should be no more than two feet. Keep the racket head above the wrist with a rigid arm and firm wrist. Accentuate your knee bend in order to hit the volley at chest level and watch the ball all the way to contact point.

sible. As the ball approaches, the arm should be held rigid, the racket firm, so that the ball rebounds off the strings. A slight modification of grip for the volley is advisable. A neutral "chopper" grip, in between the forehand and backhand grip, gives you a single-hand position for volleys on either side. We call it a "chopper" grip because it resembles the way you might hold a hammer or a hatchet. When preparing to volley, the knee bend should be accentuated, enabling you to move with greater mobility to the right or left. The racket head should be elevated on a sharp vertical diagonal, and emphasis is placed on hitting the ball as far in front of the body as possible. Although proper foot placement is not always possible in rapid-fire volleying, try at least to move your weight and shoulders into the volley. Because you are apt to have two or more volleys in a matter of seconds, you will have no time to change grips from forehand to backhand. Therefore, you must make do with one for both sides, and this takes getting used to. Regardless of your grip or position at net, try to maintain as much body balance as possible and block the ball well out in front.

EYE ON THE BALL—ALWAYS

You can't play the game unless you watch the ball. This means watching it from the moment it leaves your opponent's racket until you intercept it at the contact point. Try to see the ball hit the strings— watch it all the way. That takes a lot more effort and concentration than people think, but it's an effort that any player who wants to be good must make.

MOVEMENT AND FOOTWORK

Footwork is a vital part of every shot. Unless you are set up correctly, in the right position to stroke the ball, the shot will be ineffective. You must be able to move to the ball and adjust your position so that every shot can be hit at a comfortable level. Shots come at speeds and heights: some skid with backspin, others bound away like the American twist serve; some even slip right by you before you've gotten your racket back. But if you move quickly with short powerful steps, no bounce should fool you. You'll become accustomed to being on your toes at all times, constantly adjusting your position—turning sideways for the ground stroke, darting to net for the drop shot, moving quickly for the return of service, etcetera. Your aim should be to play every shot with your weight moving forward, meeting the ball well out in front at a convenient height. Watch the footwork of any top player and you'll notice how flexible and fluid his movements are. He's in position for every shot. This is a much-neglected aspect of stroke production, but tennis without proper movement and footwork is a sloppy proposition at best.

CAROLE: *In one of the tournaments Clark and I played together early in our relationship, the lesson of efficient footwork was impressed upon me. I was concentrating on being on my toes, jumping up and down, tense and tight, but I didn't seem to be covering much ground. Clark looked at me incredulously at one point and said: "You're doing a lot of fancy movement, but you're not going anywhere. Don't just tiptoe through the tulips, move!" The point was well taken: Movement is not vertical, but horizontal. The name of the game is going from side to side, up and back, and doing it in a hurry.*

THE DANGERS OF IMITATING FAMOUS STYLES

"Don't do as I do, do as I say." We've all been presented with that dilemma from some higher authority or expert trying to help us. One of the greatest dangers to the weekend or casual player is trying to duplicate the style of his favorite tennis star. Having spent several hours watching Rod Laver on TV, the avid fan might take to the court the next day and try to imitate his every move. Nothing could be more disastrous. Rod Laver's style is a dashing and blistering array of violent top-spin shots from all possible angles. He hits rocket shots on the dead run, from in close, off overheads, and always for the corners. He hits to win at all times, and at his best he is unbeatable. For the average player, however, these shots are foolhardy. They take years to master, even in practice, and to be able to effect them in a tense match is virtually impossible for any, save the best players in the world.

Another star, Arthur Ashe, possesses incredible timing which allows him to swing at his return of service harder than any man alive. He is uncanny in his ability to crack winners (both forehand and backhand) off even the hardest cannonball serves. He takes a full swing at the ball, and the results are astounding. An average player might connect on one out of ten with a full swing, but lacking Arthur's great timing, the return still might not be a winner.

The mercurial Rumanian, Ilie Nastase, is perhaps the most gifted player in the game. His reflexes, balance, and anticipation enable him to hit winners from impossible positions. He may strike a passing shot off the wrong foot, turned away from the net, with an uncanny flick of his wrist. His exceptional coordination allows him to volley on the run, score repeatedly, and generally pull off the most extraordinary reversals. Fellow pros are in constant awe of his natural ability, and few of us attempt the shots that are routine for Ilie. The average player would be lost attempting to duplicate Nastase's circus act.

The lessons here are clear: play within yourself. Don't attempt shots that are beyond your abilities. You have your own limitations that must dictate your style. This is true even at the highest levels. For example, young sensation Chrissy Evert realizes she lacks the big serve and volley game of Billie Jean King; yet Chrissy's excellent baseline game is good enough to put her on a par with any woman player in the world. At eighteen she lacks the power of Billie Jean King or Margaret Court, and so she relies more on her accurate ground strokes.

As your tennis improves, you may wish to become more ambitious with the variety of your strokes, but stay within your range of "percentage" shots. Every top professional has been diligently schooled in the fundamentals; the basics we recommend so strongly for you still remain the foundation of our games as well. We can hardly afford mistakes when our livelihood depends on it.

Despite appearances, we, too, play within ourselves. The difference is that we've had years to experiment and practice; so don't be lured by our example into foolhardy play at the expense of your own game.

Study any top player and you'll notice, despite whatever magic he seems to perform with his racket, that he never takes his eye off the ball, hits it late, or fails to prepare for the next shot. These are the first rules for greatness!

CLARK: *When my game goes sour, I'm in a slump, or playing well but not winning, I'll go to another pro for help. My favorite mentor is Pancho Gonzales. Pancho will watch me play or discuss my problems with me and usually between us we'll work out a solution. We all need a refresher in the basics from time to time, and in most cases it takes another trained eye to pinpoint our troubles.*

CHAPTER 4

Mixed Doubles
Tactics

Before we examine the fine points of doubles, let's take a look at some general rules. To win at doubles, whether a casual mixed game or top-flight tournament play, there is one all-important objective—to gain the offensive and hold it. The offensive or attack is predicated on controlling the net. The winners usually have their greatest moments at the net; the losers either seldom get there or function poorly when they do. Control of the DMZ, as one avid tennis fan calls the net, is vital in doubles—a game of charge and counter-charge. There is a rule of thumb that says the team which hits from up to down will beat the team which hits from down to up. It stands to reason that the team controlling the net, volleying forcefully, and hitting overheads, will keep the opponents on the defensive and be most likely to win.

Inherent in gaining the offensive is proper team-work. We discussed earlier the desirability of a compatible partner—one who also complements your game. It is not enough, however, just to play your own style, secure in the knowledge that your partner's complementary play will bail you out when your game has gone awry. This tactic ignores weaknesses that smart opponents will eventually take advantage of. A successful partnership requires team objectives, strategy, sound tactics, and practice together.

The third rule, and most eloquent in its simplicity, is the need to keep the ball in play. No matter what your proficiency, no matter what spectacular shots your daring temperament may dictate, no matter how hard you have to dig and retrieve, getting the ball back should be your primary concern. It is a largely unappreciated fact that in doubles most points are lost, not won. Errors are forced by good shots, true, but it is quite incredible how often an opponent will obligingly lose the point by simply hitting the ball out or into the net if given the chance. Most players just don't realize the importance of letting the other team make errors. In mixed doubles, at least seventy-five percent of the points are won that way.

CLARK: *One year Nancy Richey (now Gunter) and I were playing in a tournament against a Russian mixed doubles team. The match, with all its nationalistic overtones, was a very tense affair. Nancy, like her brother Cliff, is a fierce competitor, and she was playing magnificently. In my eagerness to carry the day, I was trying my fanciest and most daring shots. The only trouble was that none were going in. I went from bad to worse. I was terrible. Finally Nancy turned to me and said in a rather curt voice: "Clark, just get the damn ball in the court; I'll do the rest!" I did manage to get a few more in, and she did do the rest! We won. This illustrates the importance of keeping the ball in play and not giving away points through foolish play. Good percentage tennis is winning tennis.*

MENTAL AWARENESS

Under this heading come the elements of concentration, strategy changes, and communication. Concentration, following the ball on every point, and keeping a keen competitive edge are absolute necessities. The slightest lapse can turn a match completely around. Thinking quickly and decisively is a condition of awareness and concentration, not a born trait. At the top level of any sport, where there is little difference in abilities, it is usually the powers of concentration that determine the winners. At the club level where abilities vary greatly, good concentration can be a huge plus. Many players just don't make the mental effort necessary to stay in command of the match. Thinking on your feet pays off handsomely.

As the match progresses, be prepared to change tactics. Reviewing the situation and studying mistakes to determine your own and opponents' weaknesses is smart tennis. Communication between two partners is also necessary; working as a team requires verbal help. The partner best able to judge the flight of the ball should yell "out," "good," "Drop it," (etcetera), on questionable shots. On overheads, if there's any doubt, a "mine" or "yours" as the case dictates will prevent collisions or a complete miss. A weak lob requires a "back" call, or seeing a drop shot early, your prompt "up" call will help your partner.

It should be obvious to you by now that mixed doubles is not just a hit and giggle proposition. There is a certain science to the game, and it requires all the cunning and concentration you can muster. In the following chapters we'll discuss specific strategy and tactics, noting helpful rules that will allow you to better understand the game in its fascinating complexities.

THE SERVE

We've mentioned that successful doubles is predicated on taking and holding the net. Aggressive net play is a winning doubles tactic, and the serve provides the best means of getting to the net and holding the offensive. Originally the service was only a means of getting the ball in play. In modern tennis it is the single most potent shot, and its advantage should not be ignored. In doubles, getting the first serve in is of the utmost importance. Inasmuch as the server is expected to advance to the net, a hard smash is not always the best tactic. A hard first serve that rarely goes in or is followed by a weak second serve is a set-up for the opposition. Even a weaker woman can step up on a short weak second serve and make a forceful return, allowing her team to gain offensive. The first serve should be a controlled spin or slice deep, preferably to the backhand. This "kick" serve gives the server more time to advance to the net in a position parallel with his partner. The proper position for mixed doubles service is shown in Figure 1. The server stands midway between the center of the baseline and the sideline, leaving the shortest distance to the desired net position. The server's partner stations himself at the net far enough away so that a swing of the racket will not touch the net. He must guard the alley as well as shots hit at him. The return will usually be cross court away from the net man—an easier shot for the charging server to pick up.

The American twist service with its big hop is a

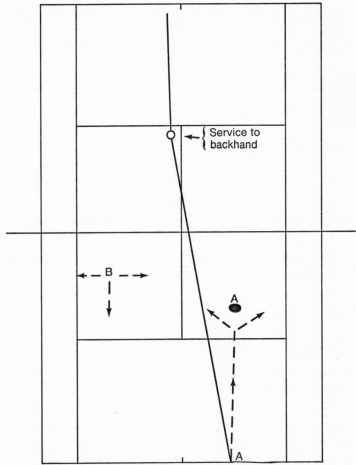

Service to
backhand

B

A

A

Fig. 1: **STANDARD SERVICE POSITIONS**

most difficult ball to return, especially when delivered
deep to the backhand. The woman need only attain a
reasonably deep serve along this pattern, and the
team's attacking proficiency should equal that of the
man's service. Regardless of which partner is serving,
however, consistency in getting the first one in is the

key. Otherwise you lose your service advantage and
may even tire yourself out running to net on faults.
A good first service should go in four out of five times.
The receiver is never allowed to get set and gobble up
a weak second serve. Psychologically the opponents
are off balance for consistently successful first serves,
and their returns are apt to be weak or defensive.

After initiating the attack with the serve, and
advancing to net, the partners should move up and
back together. If the serve has been deep to the backhand, there is little chance the receiver will try to pass
the net man down the alley. There are two reasons:
the backhand is usually the weaker side for both men
and women; and, secondly, the margin for error on
such a difficult shot is pronounced. The receiver can ill
afford to run around his backhand purely on the
chance he may be able to "smoke" one by the opposition. He'd be badly out of position for any return.

The server should make every effort to reach the
service line for his first volley. This requires a series
of quick long steps right after the serve. As he reaches
the service line he should pause, gain his balance
(bringing his feet parallel to the net), and move toward the return. He should be prepared to change direction, as the return may be a low cross-court chip,
too difficult to volley, or a floater that gives the server
more time to further advance to net and hit for a
winner.

At this point your eyes should never leave the ball.
Resist the temptation to peek at your opponents—the
shot invariably comes a cropper after that indulgence.
The first volley is the most important. It need not be
an outright winner, but it must put the opponents on

the defensive. So watch that ball, and at least make good contact.

CLARK: *Several years ago, Anne Jones and I were playing in the mixed doubles final of the French championships. Anne has a fine first serve and good ground strokes, but her volleying is sometimes inconsistent. We had won the first set and Anne was serving for the match in the second set. I suggested she concentrate especially hard on her first volley, placing it deep down the middle. I felt she must volley effectively after her good serve. We had our opponents in a hole, and this game could win it all. All we needed was some good deep volleying from Anne if our opponents returned her serve. Well, Anne performed exactly according to form. She hit four excellent first serves, but we lost the game at love. In her eagerness to finish off the match, Anne either mis-hit or misplayed ALL four volleys on the return of service. After losing that game, we lost the match and the title which should have been ours. This is a perfect example of the necessity for strong first volleys from the service team. Also it shows the unexpected reversals that occur when the receiving team gets the serve back at all costs.*

THE POACH

The net man has several options open to him. He may hold his ground, awaiting his partner's first volley, or he may indulge in that intoxicating venture called the poach. Briefly, poaching means crossing over to your partner's side of the court to cut off the anticipated cross-cut return. If the return is a weak floater within your reach, begging to be volleyed away, it is entirely permissable and indeed desirable to take that liberty. Be aggressive. Remember, the offensive is control of the net. Women should feel no hesitancy in making this shot. Their anticipation and mobility at net is as important as the man's. The poach catches the opposition off guard, and in many cases the net man's closeness to the net enables him to put the ball away—often difficult for the charging server. If the net man moves quickly, watches the ball closely, and intercepts it out in front, the poach is a very effective shot. The poach is also a good psychological weapon. The very fact that it is being used places a burden on the receiver. He becomes uncertain as to where to hit his return and may succumb to the fatal error of watching his opponents rather than the ball. At times, when you are not going to poach, a slight feint (head jerk, racket shift, or half step to the other side) may create indecision in the receiver's mind and lead to a poor return or no return at all. The server must remember, however, that his partner at the net is the boss. If the net man poaches, he doesn't have time to look back to check the server's position. But the partner coming to net can change directions and cover the vacated area as in Figure 2. If the net man moves right to intercept a weak return, the server moves left to cover for him. Remember, however, never to dawdle in the middle of the court watching the beauty of your partner's lightning-fast poach. Get to the other side fast and be ready to join the action if a return comes your way. The poach is not a fool-proof tactic, and there's nothing quite as foolish as both partners standing on one side of the court as an angled shot speeds by them on the

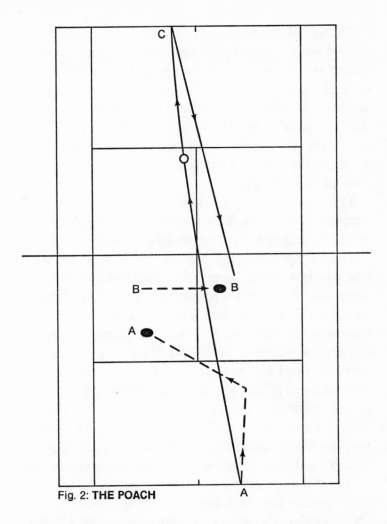

Fig. 2: **THE POACH**

opposite side. The poach provides a perfect example of the need for teamwork, teamwork, teamwork.

UNCONVENTIONAL SERVICE FORMATIONS

Occasionally the need may arise for a change in service strategy. Perhaps a weaker partner may be having difficulty holding service or the opposition may simply be just a little better in every category, and although you're still in the match, you just can't seem to win enough games. A change in tactics to keep your opponents off balance will often improve the situation. An element of surprise is a cunning move when things seem darkest. The entire match can be reversed sometimes by the simplest change. Let's look at an application for the service.

The Australian formation (Figure 3) realigns the server and net man. This is extremely effective if the weaker partner is serving and finds that in the conventional formation the receiver is returning service powerfully—either deep to the backhand or with too much cross-court pace, preventing an effective volley. This Australian alignment with server and net man on the same side allows a stronger net player to protect the weaker server's backhand. He has the chance to cover more of the net, and with a little anticipation can intercept all but the most accurate returns aimed at his crossing partner. After serving, the server crosses immediately to the opposite court. The server now has the option of playing an easier forehand volley or forehand ground stroke. A stronger stroke is utilized and the receiver is now required to change both the direction and pace of the ball if he wishes to continue playing the weaker serving opponent. Chances are the receiver won't know where to hit the ball, for a while at least. In adapting, he may lose valuable momentum or perhaps lose his timing altogether. So, you see, a simple element of surprise may well throw the opponents into confusion from which they won't recover.

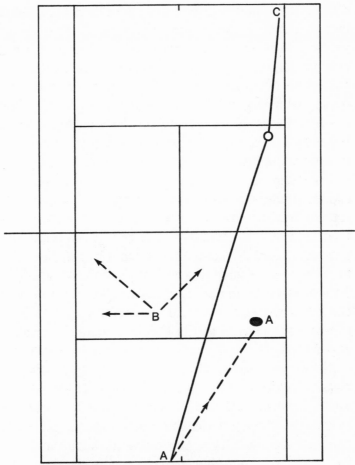

Fig. 3: **AUSTRALIAN SERVICE POSITION**

Sadly, when we contemplate errors in tennis, we must also consider blatant weaknesses that may sabotage even the best teamwork. Most common among weekend players is a weak serve and the inability to follow the net. The procedure of striking an accurate forcing serve and following it quickly to net, all the while maintaining your balance and control, is no mean feat. The best professionals in the world have spent years perfecting that sequence. It's an act that's not always easy to duplicate; it doesn't come easily, and some may never master it. If you can't, don't be discouraged. There are alternatives, and although they are less desirable, they may be the answer for you. If you don't play often enough to get that first serve in, or it's woefully weak when you do and the opposition is belting every offering right by your net partner as you struggle to get to net, there is a last resort: retreat (rather than be annihilated). It is generally true in such circumstances that one of the team is a more confident stroke-maker. From the baseline he'll be able to take advantage of more time in which to cover the court and perhaps hit a forcing shot that will allow you both to advance to the net. In Figure 4, both partners are aligned at the baseline while the weaker partner serves. Now the server need not rush the net on the serve, and he should also be better prepared to play the return. This is a delaying tactic, however, and should be used only to better prepare the team to charge net. With practice and less pressure over rushing the net on serve, the service should improve enough to allow another attempt at the classic serve-and-volley approach to doubles.

CHANGES AT THE END OF A SET

Many players don't realize that changes in service order and court side are permitted at the end of a set. For example, if your serve has been "off" in the first set, perhaps your partner should open the second set, even if by the initial order of service it's still your

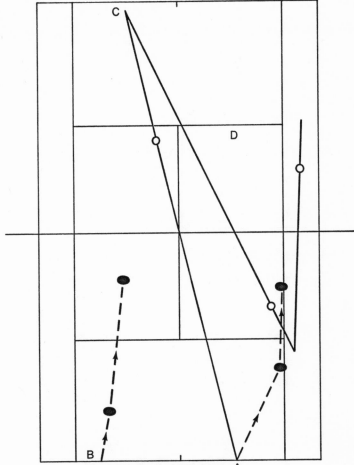

Fig. 4: **DEEP SERVICE ALIGNMENT**

serve. Your partner's serve may not be as strong as yours, but if the team is losing on your serve, a change of serving order may be a winning strategy. By the same token, if one of you is experiencing difficulty returning service on a particular side, change courts at the end of the set. Never pig-headedly stick to a

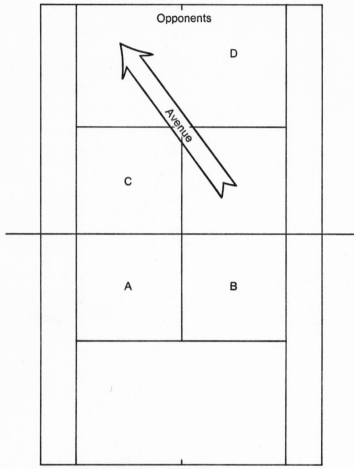

Fig. 5: **THE AVENUE OF ATTACK**

losing alignment on the assumption that, "it's just a question of time; it will come." Normally, the added pressure of feeling inadequate or frustrated in what you know should be a better performance will just make the situation worse as the match progresses. A change gives you a better chance to regain your timing and strokes.

THE AVENUE OF ATTACK

So far, we've seen the need to move together, control the net, put the first serve in play and generally act as a team. Implied in these tactics is the proposition that by so doing you will disrupt or split your opponent's teamwork. There is a premise in doubles that if you can split the opposition, one up, one back, or one behind the other, your avenues of attack are greatly increased. Your own teamwork and harmonious movements provide the base from which to attack your opponents' misalignment. In Figure 5, the split opposition provides the attacking team with a clear and easy avenue of attack. There is little the opponents can do to remedy this predicament once the attackers are in control of the net. So keep in mind the need to move together and create in your opponents this fatal opening. After the serve, almost all the shots in doubles are designed either to create this opening or take advantage of it. These shots and more basic strategy will be discussed in the following chapter.

CHAPTER 5

The Return of Service and Baseline Strategy

Every stroke is important in tennis, but the return of service is considered by many the single most important shot in doubles. Even if you win all your service games, you still must break your opponents at least once a set to win. The return of service is a most difficult shot to play effectively and consistently. If your return is weak or erratic, you just don't stand much chance of winning. You may have excellent strokes—cross-court forehands, strong backhands, punishing overheads—but if you miss the return, you'll never have a chance to display your form. Therefore, you must concentrate on the return from the moment the ball leaves the server's racket, and adjust your stroke and footwork to meet the serve.

The receiver must return the serve at all costs. Many a point has been won on the worst returns because the serving team made a simple error. So don't go for winners off the serve. The shot is just too hard to hit. Make the other team win the point; don't give it to them. Generally you should return the serve cross-court, safely away from the net man, looking for the opportunity to take the net and gain the offensive. You need not "kill" the ball but rather direct it to an area that the incoming server will find difficult to play. For receiving service, stand on your toes, in a ready position, knees bent with your weight slightly forward. Hold your racket in front, cradled in the left hand at the throat. Be ready to bring back the racket and turn your body as soon as you see whether the serve is coming to your forehand or backhand. On most serves you probably won't have time to take a full swing so use a limited backswing and come forward on the shot.

The receiver has a tough task against a strong serving team. A high bounding twist deep to the backhand is tough in any league. You must keep your eye on the ball, an eye on the net man to see if he's going to poach, an eye on the server to see where he's going to position himself, and at the same time make a split-second decision on what type of return to hit. It's small wonder the return is called the toughest shot in tennis.

POSITION FOR RETURN

Because the receiving team is endeavoring to force the serving team to make defensive volleys, the first consideration for the receiver is to return the ball as quickly as possible. This entails moving a step or two in front of the baseline in order to intercept the serve on the rise and send it back low before the server has a chance to advance too far toward net. If the server is forced to hit his first volley off balance from below the level of the net, the receiving team has a greater chance to gain the offensive. A return that lands at the feet of the advancing server gives the receiving team every opportunity to win the point. On the other hand, a floater that drifts across the net is pure gravy for the service team. The closer in the receiver, the better the chance he has to angle his return cross court, and that

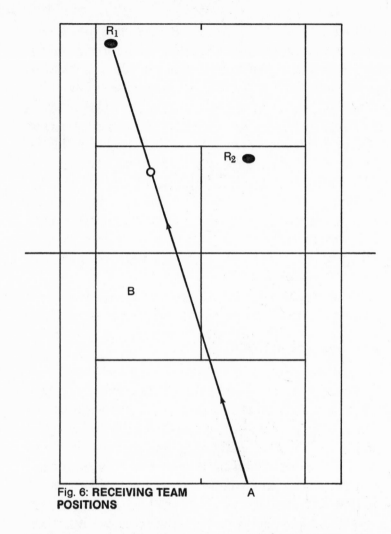

Fig. 6: **RECEIVING TEAM POSITIONS**

much more opportunity to get to net himself. The receiver positions himself inside the baseline on a straight line from the server through the service court (Figure 6). Depending on the strength of the serve he faces, the receiver may be forced to move back to the baseline or be able to move in even closer. Under no circumstances should the ball be allowed to drop below the peak of its bounce. This would be making the shot tougher for you as well as giving the server more time to charge net. On the second serve the receiver can move in an additional step or two. Very often women forget to do this in mixed doubles, perferring to take a bigger swing at the slower second serve without changing positions. This is asking for trouble. Remember, you're trying to get the serve back at the server's feet, so move in and cut it off. Even the most brutish men are tied up by the controlled return at the feet. It's like eating peas with a knife—pure agony.

In Figure 7, the desired target area for the return is designated. The return should be cross court and, again, must be low. As we mentioned, you need only meet the serve; speed is of secondary importance. There is another advantage to the "blocked" or "chipped" cross-court return of service. Not only does it force the server to volley up, but it also forces him to supply much of the pace on the volley from his own stroke. He'll be stumbling around, trying to hit a forceful shot from his shoe tops. Occasionally, you may wish to gamble and swing for an outright winner. This flat drive is best used off a flat cannonball serve and catches the server far back in the court. If struck well, the hard return is a glamorous stroke, but beware of the dangers of overswinging and driving the ball out or into the net. You should really be "on" your game before swinging away regularly. The odds just aren't on your side. Another alternative is a drive

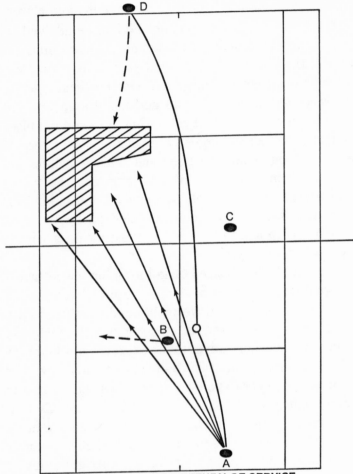

Fig. 7: **TARGET AREA FOR RETURN OF SERVICE**

either right at the net man or down the alley. These are risky shots and require good pace and accuracy. But as a surprise it is a good tactic and keeps the serving team off balance. When you're playing the forehand, it's a good opportunity to try a drive down the

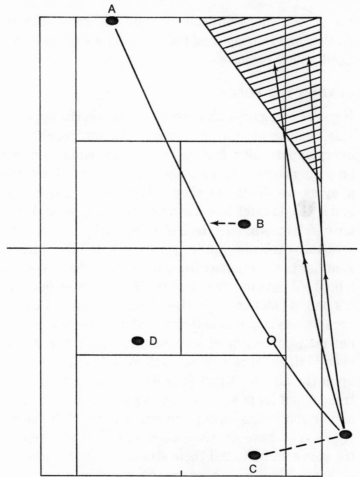

Fig. 8: **RETURN OF SERVICE DOWN THE ALLEY**

alley. More than likely, the opposing net man will be leaning toward the center which exposes his backhand alley. When you're pulled wide by the serve, your target area opens up considerably down the line (Figure 8). The same is true for the backhand side, but the shot is more difficult as your backhand may be weaker and the opposing net man is in a stronger forehand volley position.

BEATING THE POACH

If you're up against an expert net man on the opposite side, chances are he'll be all over the net, poaching at every opportunity. Naturally if you anticipate a poach on your return, the best shot is the drive down the alley as we discussed above. This keeps him honest and if you do catch him when he's crossing, your shot is an outright winner. He looks the fool to boot, and probably he'll be more restrained in the future. Another tactic against strong net play is the use of the lob.(We'll devote more time to this shot later because it's one of the most effective shots in tennis.) Briefly, here its use is obvious. If you can't get the ball by the net man on return of service, you surely can get it over him. By throwing the ball over his head (get it up in the air; don't just fade it), you force him to retreat when he is most set at the net. The advancing server must also change direction completely to retrieve. You have deprived them of the first volley off the serve and blunted their attack. In their confusion or haste, they may even collide while going after it (Figure 9). The lob should be hit high and deep over the net man's head unless the server's advance to net is so reckless that he is unable to reverse his direction.

In sum, the best rule for return of service is, "Mix it up." Variety and surprise are most valuable for the receiver, especially against a strong serving team. Make them think; make them move; make them reach;

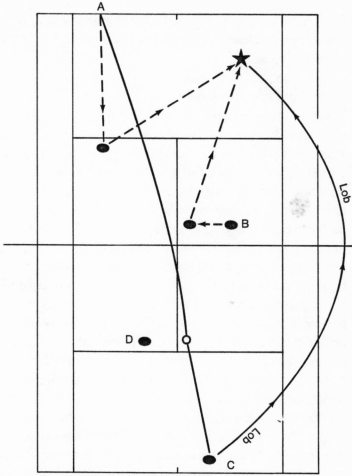

Fig. 9: **LOB RETURN OF SERVICE**

and always be alert to move in and steal the offensive from them.

THE RECEIVER'S PARTNER

In these days of aggressive doubles, the receiver's partner generally plays a modified net position. He should position himself several feet inside the service line, slightly closer to the center line than the alley. This may seem like a vulnerable position at first glance; i.e., in "no man's land" (the middle of the court), and easy prey for the server's first volley. But, because the receiving team is attempting to gain the offensive, he must be there to capitalize on a possible weak first volley by the serving team. If the receiver's return is weak, the point will most likely be lost anyway no matter where you are. You're better off anticipating the serving team's first volley and moving in. This requires watching your partner's return only long enough to determine its direction and then shifting your attention quickly to the service team. Some players watch only the opponent's eyes to determine the path of the return. If the opposing net man moves to poach, you can move to counter. If you see the server falter in an attempt to dig out a low return, move in and pinch off the shot. You need only move a few feet to cut off his volley and your return catches both server and net man off guard (Figure 10). The receiver's partner must be alert, however; he must anticipate and be alert for that weak first volley from the server. If he's flat footed or slow, he becomes easy prey when both opponents are up at net and his partner is still back.

If, by chance, the opposing server fails to advance to net after his serve (lazy!), the receiver should attempt to hit his return deep and follow it in. His partner in the modified net position now has an excellent opportunity to move in further and hit a winning volley. The tables have been reversed and he suddenly becomes the poacher or aggressor—simply because

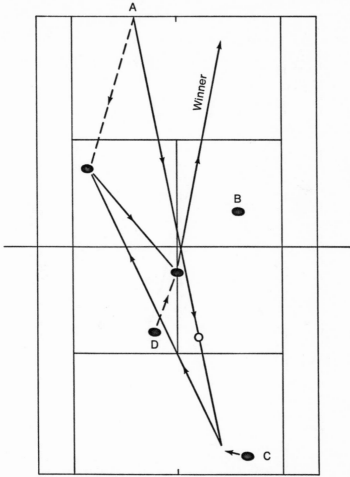

Fig. 10: **MODIFIED NET MAN VOLLEYS FOR WINNERS**

the server failed to follow his serve to net. The serving team has been caught with one up and one back, opening the clear avenue of attack (Figure 11). They are unable to defend against the cross-court volley. The opposition has been split, and your team is the winner.

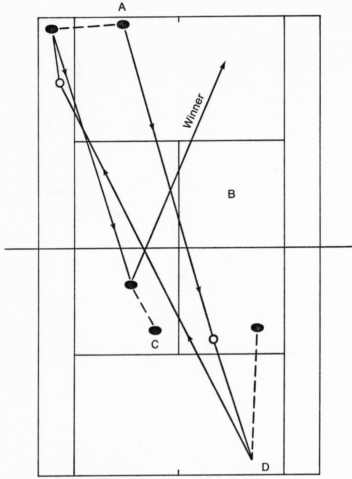

Fig. 11: **SERVER FAILS TO COME TO NET**

TWO DEEP RECEIVERS

Occasionally it may be necessary to alter the receiving team's position, moving the modified net man back to the baseline. This tactic should be used only when the opponent's service is so strong that the receiver is unable to make any but the weakest return which is being consistently volleyed away for winners. This is not an uncommon occurrence in mixed doubles where the discrepancy in abilities may be significant. Rather than trying to weather a storm of punishing first volleys from the serving team, the modified net man can, instead, retrieve and assist his partner from the baseline (Figure 12). Again, however, this tactic should be used only as a means to help you eventually get back to net. Remember, doubles is a game of attack and it's impossible to control the net from the baseline.

BASELINE STRATEGY

Assuming you have been forced to retreat to the baseline for one reason or another, there are several ways to get back to net or make your "counter-charge." Your predicament is not favorable under any circumstances, but with sound stroke production there is always hope.

THE LOB

How glamorous the leaping player looks as he intercepts the lob with a crunching sweep of his racket! Well, it's a simple fact that most tennis players can't hit an overhead with any real power or consistency.

The lob is one of the most underrated weapons in tennis. It gives the weaker team plenty of time to maneuver and requires the other team to hit a more difficult shot—the overhead. When you're both back or badly out of position, a wise tactic is the defensive lob, i.e., a high, deep lob that requires the opponent to bounce the ball or take a real risk in striking on the fly a vertically descending ball. The defensive lob

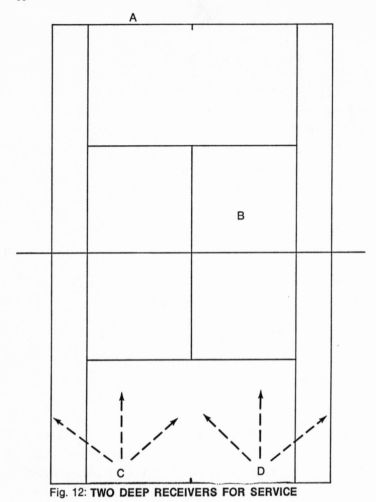

Fig. 12: **TWO DEEP RECEIVERS FOR SERVICE**

gives your team time to maneuver back into an offensive position before the return is made. You may
have noticed that one or the other of your opponents
has more difficulty in hitting overheads. If so, lob to
that side. They may choose to change positions to
enable the stronger partner to hit the lob, but chances

are that the resultant confusion and hurrying to adjust will produce a mediocre shot. If your opponents are literally right on top of the net, you may use the offensive or topspin lob. This lob has less height and is designed to just clear their reach and carry deeper with less arc and topspin. It's a difficult shot to hit, however, and is an easy put away for the opponents if you fail to clear them. If in doubt, always hit the lob high enough to ensure that the opposition will at least have to run back in order to return it. Don't forget the sun and the wind either. Let your opponents get a good dose of the ball silhouetted against the sun. They'll be seeing spots or dashing around to avoid looking into the sun for quite a while. Always take notice, too, of which way the wind is blowing before you lob. It's most frustrating to hit what you consider to be a perfect lob, only to see it sail wide or long.

CLARK: *No matter who my mixed doubles partner, no matter what her skills, I have always stressed one rule whenever she's in trouble or in doubt about what type of shot to hit: lob, lob, lob. I've bludgeoned that into Carole a thousand times if I've done it once. It's the one shot in tennis where a woman can be on an absolute par with the men. It should be used often.*

THE DROP SHOT

Rather than attempting to belt the ball by the net man from the baseline (dangerous tactic unless you are exceptionally accurate), for variation try the "drop," "touch," or "drink" shot. This is a softer angled shot that just clears the net and forces the opponents to volley up. Your team is now able to countercharge the

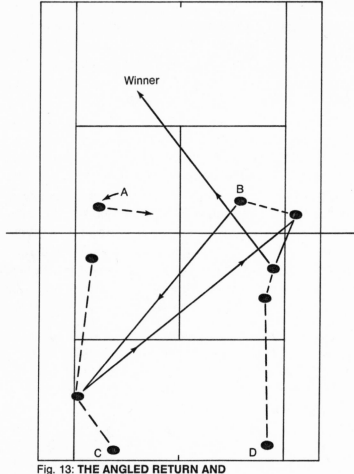

**Fig. 13: THE ANGLED RETURN AND
COUNTER CHARGE**

net and you have the chance to intercept his rising
volley and hit a winner (Figure 13). This is a perfect
example of seizing the offensive, not by use of power,
but by guile. Women whose strokes may not be strong
enough to overpower their opponents can use such
"touch" shots to set up their partners for the surprise

kill—a perfect example of how good teamwork pays off, and a most demoralizing turnabout for the opponents!

In summary, going from the defensive posture of a receiving team to the offensive or control of the net requires the cunning and imaginative use of the drive, lob, and touch returns. Using any one shot to the exclusion of others will soon backfire when your opponents realize your predictability. It's wise to mix up your attack; keep the opponents off balance by using all your shots. After all, you're trying to upset their timing and teamwork. If they are to hold the offensive, at least make them work for the advantage. When you accomplish this variety in shotmaking, you are playing the game in all its style—as it is supposed to be played—a real challenge.

NET PLAY AND THE OVERHEAD

You have gathered by now that the volley is by far the winningest shot in doubles. Playing the net effectively is the best formula for winning. We've discussed net play by the service and receiving team only through the first volley. For subsequent shots, there are several basic rules governing play when both teams have advanced to net. Your team must be positioned so as to best cover the net and also protect against the lob. In mixed doubles, the man, because of his longer reach and stride, may wish to cover slightly more of the court. Let us assume that the man is playing the "ad" court (lefthand court). This enables him to better utilize his forehand power for lobs and shots down the middle.

CLARK: *There are exceptions to every rule, and some exceptions confound the experts. In men's doubles, I normally play the forehand or deuce court. And a switch to the backhand or ad court in mixed doubles has not always been an immediate reaction for me. As a matter of fact, I was an exception in the 1972 Wimbeldon mixed doubles semi-final. Billie Jean King and I were teamed against Ilie Nastase and Rosie Casals in what was to be a real dogfight. Before the match, Billie Jean decided I should play the forehand court. She likes the backhand side and reasoned that my greater familiarity with the forehand side would give our team the advantage. I concurred, as Billie Jean is a fine volleyer and has a good overhead. She's also a hard gal to dissuade when she has made up her mind about something, and had I balked at her suggestion (or was it a demand?) our partnership might have ended right there. In any case we strode onto the center court confident of victory. Alas, so did our opponents. Someone in our match was going to have to come in second. But our strategy for the match with me playing the forehand had one catch: We won the toss, elected to serve, and there across the net was Ilie Nastase playing the forehand court—the side that he too is most accustomed to! They were an exception to the rule also. It was a seesaw battle which, I'm sorry to say, we lost. (Maybe I should have played the backhand court....)*

Depending on the changing position of the ball, the team moves continually—in close, to one side, drifting back, et cetera. The standard position (Figure 14) aligns the team within ten feet of the net and as close as possible toward the center while still guarding the

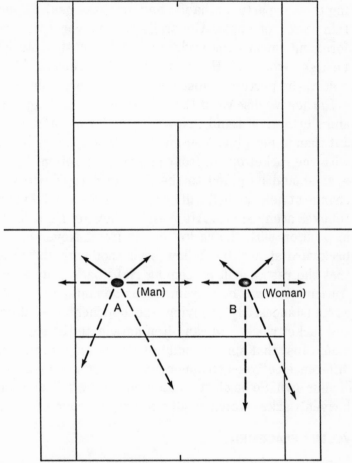

Fig. 14: **NET POSITION**

alleys. This puts you well into the service court. Don't make the mistake of standing on the alley line, because most winners from close quarters are hit down the middle. You're close enough to cut off the angle shots so you must protect against the middle attack. As you move the net, it helps to have an understanding of your partner's habits and an agreement on certain types of shots. Generally the player with the forehand toward the middle will take most shots hit between you and the majority of overheads. If in doubt, the partners must yell, "yours," or, "mine."

Earlier we discussed the importance of anticipation and alertness in tennis. Nowhere is this more important than in net play. You must be poised, knees bent, with the racket out in front in a ready position. Your eyes should be glued to the ball. In a rapid-fire exchange at net, the ball will be by you in a second if your reflexes aren't sharp. After each volley get right back in position with the racket out in front. Never move backward at net, but follow each shot with the idea that the return will be coming right back your way. Anticipation can be a tremendous advantage in such circumstances. By studying the opponent's position and racket work, you can often anticipate the shot he plans. Just that split-second advantage may mean the difference between an opponent's winner and a winner of your own. So be alert; get a jump on the ball, and for heaven's sake, watch it all the way to your strings.

VOLLEY PLACEMENT

The basic objective of the attacking net team is to force the opponents to hit from down to up, i.e., a defensive shot. You are then in a position to volley for an outright winner, having the jump on a weak rising shot from the opponents. Your first volley, however, may not always be so advantageous. In such cases, it's good to remember that a succession of shots may be required to win the point. The strokes at your disposal are numerous; we'll discuss those that are most effective. A good general rule dictates that the first

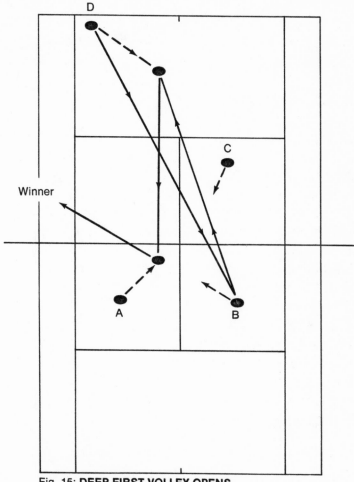

Fig. 15: **DEEP FIRST VOLLEY OPENS COURT FOR WINNER**

volley should be hit deep down the middle. This is true for both service team and receiving team. The deep volley should be hit with pace and as low as possible. It is not always a winning shot but it puts the opponents on the defensive, and opens up the court for a second volley angled to the side for a winner. (Figure 15). Once you have succeeded in driving your oppo-

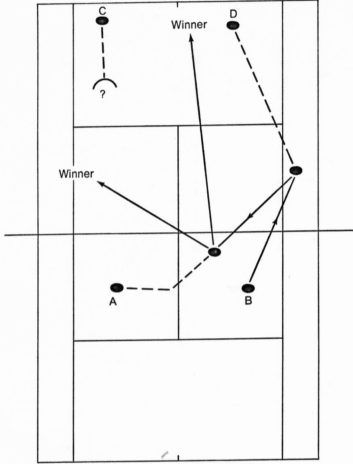

Fig. 16: **ANGLE OR DROP VOLLEY OPENS COURT FOR WINNER**

nents to the baseline, by lobs or deep volleying, then try the angle volley or drop volley. If your opponents retrieve these placements, then counter again with the deep volley. It is a system of thrust and parry. The idea is to move the opponents up, back, and to the side until they are divided, providing you with a clear avenue of attack for a winner (Figure 16). "Divide and conquer."

Because the net is six inches lower in the middle than on the sides and the court is longer than it is wide, the deep volley down the middle is a better percentage shot, especially for the first volley. Likewise, if you're in trouble and your opponents seem to have the upper hand at net, try some soft or angled volleys over the center of the net where it's lowest. Rather than hitting up in a defensive manner, angle sharply a shot that barely clears the net. Your opponents, in turn, must either bounce the ball or volley up. In effect, you are sparring with the opponents until you can create that opening for a winner.

Remember that the game of doubles is at its best when all four participants are at the net exchanging shots, using all their guile and shotmaking ability.

THE "ACHILLES HEEL" OR OVERHEAD

A word here about playing the lob is necessary for the successful mixed doubles team. It's a sad fact that most weekend or club players are far from proficient in overhead play. For some reason, probably the irregularity with which the lob is used, most players aren't too concerned about missing the overhead. If they miss a forehand, they are furious; if an easy volley is netted, they are distraught. But a blown overhead is just ignored—somehow not really a part of tennis. These players have missed a golden opportunity to win points. Many men swing wildly at the ball, more satisfied with the sound and power of the smash than its direction or result. Invariably they take their eye off the ball and the shot fails. More often than not, a sly grin appears on their faces as if to say, "Well, I really cracked that one, didn't I? If it had gone over, you'd be dead!" The message is clear: Pick a spot where you want to hit the shot, watch the ball closely, forget your opponents, and be satisfied with making firm contact. You should also make every effort to hit overheads before they bounce, rather than retreating to the baseline.

As we suggested earlier, it's advantageous for the man to play the ad court utilizing his greater reach and forehand power on lobs hit down the middle. In some cases, he may cross to the woman's side to hit the overhead if the angle of his shot will be better than hers. Agreement on this type of shot before play is the best bet, however. The man must beware of getting dangerously out of position while chasing down a lob on his partner's side. Women have been known to hit some very potent overheads of their own.

CHAPTER 6

Fitness
and Practice

We've covered a lot so far: mixed doubles philosophy, teamwork, strokes, tactics, and strategy. It may not be easy to digest all of it at one sitting. Our advice is to take a little at a time, concentrating on whatever amount you can handle until it becomes second nature on the court. We have no instant formula for success, but there are some considerations that can speed up the process and make tennis a more rewarding game.

FITNESS

The old adage that exercise keeps you young and healthy is heard often for one simple reason: it's true. Sensible physical activity is an important part of our lives, and tennis provides one of the most enjoyable means to stay fit. It is truly a game for a lifetime. (We've seen toddlers of three years on the court and older players active well into their seventies.) You may need some help to keep your tennis fitness. Ideally, playing every day is the most enjoyable and productive way to keep you and your game in shape. Nothing sharpens reflexes or improves fitness for the game as well as just playing regularly. Alas, this is not always possible for the weekend player. But there are other ways to keep fit for tennis and help your game as well.

Getting in shape before you step on the court will make your tennis that much more rewarding. Even the best players on the international circuit supplement their tennis with a regimen of exercises and running. The demands on their fitness are extreme, and a tired or out-of-shape athlete is a loser in any sport. No matter how casual the game, it helps to be in shape. Stamina is always a big consideration. Although doubles does not require the same speed afoot as singles, it does demand good mobility and quickness. We're not going to advocate a spartan training regime; that's overdoing it. But some exercises and training approaches are helpful for any player.

There has been much emphasis in recent years on the benefits of running. Whether a special aerobics program or easy jogging, the activity is good for the heart, lungs, and legs. As distasteful as it may be to some, running will help your tennis. But if that's not your style, at least walk up stairs (rather than using elevators) and walk short distances whenever possible.

Don't sit at a desk all week and expect to tear around the tennis court like Rod Laver on the weekends, especially if you've had no exercise in the interim. If you're tired after only a set, then you're not in shape to play good tennis. More than likely you'll stop following your serve to net and fail to move quickly under lobs. If that's the case, you're cheating your partner and yourself. A little effort in your spare time goes a long way when it's five–all in the third set.

Here are some other exercises we recommend for keeping your tennis fitness. A light regimen of jumping jacks, jogging in place, bending and stretching exercises are all good. Especially effective are those exercises concentrating on the stomach muscles. Sit-ups and leg-lifts are excellent. For men, start with twenty-five a day and work up in weekly increments of five. For women, lie on your back, raise your feet four or five inches off the ground and swing each leg individually from side to side, stretching all those stomach and side muscles. You'll improve your figure as well as your tennis fitness. Use your imagination in exercising and you'll be surprised how interesting and challenging training can become. Because arm and wrist strength is necessary in the tennis stroke, any exercise that develops those muscles is desirable. Squeezing a squash ball, tennis ball, or hand gripper develops both the wrist and forearm. This can be done any time during the day. For instance, with ten or fifteen minutes of unobtrusive squeezing on the way to work every day, your strength will increase considerably.

For agility and quickness afoot, skipping rope is an ideal exercise. Select a heavy rope long enough to clear your head by a foot. Vary your style as you jump changing from one foot to the other or both feet. Done properly this exercise develops arm strength as well as improving your timing and balance.

Exercise, like tennis, demands concentration and diligence. Just going through the motions is not enough. Your body should be challenged; you should be winded and tired after exercise—an indication that you have exerted yourself. Be sensible, however. If you're over forty and exercise irregularly, take it easy until you establish a suitable regimen. Don't adopt an

Olympics athlete's training schedule at first, and if there's any doubt about your program, consult a doctor for approval. More than likely he'll applaud both the game and exercises for your general health and fitness.

Except on the very hottest of summer days it is advisable to wear a sweater as you warm up. Once you're loose and your muscles unkinked, shed the warm-up gear. After playing, always put the sweater back on or your muscles may stiffen when you cool off.

Tennis, like any exercise, requires a well-balanced diet. This does not mean a large meal before playing nor does a light breakfast carry you through a full day of tennis. You should leave yourself at least an hour to digest before playing and on weekends, when you're apt to play both mornings and afternoons, a light lunch is sufficient. Of more importance is the consumption of fluids to replace those lost through perspiration. Gargantuan intakes of soft drinks will only slow you down. Take a swallow or two of liquids quite often during play: water, tea, orange juice, or other thirst quenchers. On especially hot days a salt tablet may be required to keep your salt level up.

In general the rules for fitness in tennis come down to common sense and preparation. If you are to run well on the court, you must run whenever possible; if you are endeavoring to strengthen your volleys, you must improve your quickness, timing, and wrist strength; if you are to maintain your energy, you must eat sensibly. The above suggestions and examples are indicative of the little things you can do to improve your tennis through better fitness.

PRACTICE

Now we come to the most underrated, most misunderstood, and most unpopular aspect of tennis for the average player: practice. Almost all players want to improve; but most either won't practice or approach practice incorrectly. For the player who expects to improve with a friendly game once a week, but can't understand his inability to do so, there is a simple answer: all play and no work makes for static tennis. Practice can be hard work, and consequently few players are willing to make the effort. But it's great exercise and most satisfying because it's invariably rewarded by improvement. Perfecting a stroke against the backboard for fifteen minutes a day is worth far more than five sets spent repeating the same old errors. Practice, like actual play, demands your full attention. You should attempt to return every ball on the first bounce whether banging against a backboard or rallying with your spouse. Be intelligent in your practice. If your backhand is weak, don't keep running around it to show off your crushing forehand. You may impress the onlookers but only until an opponent hits a drive to your backhand side. Take pains in your warm-up or practice sessions to hit the shots that give you trouble; make every stroke count. This is especially true for those who don't have the opportunity to play regularly.

Here are some brief practice principles with helpful hints for men and women. Don't make these sessions marathon affairs, but rather take one drill at a time and give it your full concentration for a designated period. Rome wasn't built in a day, and you're not going to get to Forest Hills overnight. But sensible practice, even if only done sporadically, will improve your game considerably.

GROUND STROKES

Concentrate on grooving this stroke. Remember, always take the racket back early with a firm wrist and hit *through* the ball. Place targets in the corner of the court and try to hit them during rallies. Practice cross-court drives and down-the-line drives, keeping score with your practice partner. As your confidence builds, have your opponent move to net and hit the same cross-courts and down-the-lines at him. The speeded-up returns will improve your movement, footwork, and balance. Common errors to guard against are: wristiness, hitting the ball late off the wrong foot, not bending the knees for low balls, and taking your eye off the ball while pulling your head up.

Women: We've noticed that one of the most frequent mistakes women make in mixed doubles is allowing the ball to drop too low. In doubles it is imperative to take the ball at its highest point in the bounce or on the rise if possible.

Men: Resist the temptation to overswing at what seems to be a fat ground stroke. In doubles, placement rather than speed is of primary importance.

THE SERVICE

Strive for consistency in your service. Practice the slice and kick serves since they provide greater control with as much depth as a flat cannonball. In early stages of practice, aim for corners of the court using boxes as targets. As you gain more proficiency, enlist an opponent to return your serve as you follow it in to net. You don't want to develop the service in isolation from the first volley which is so critical in doubles. Common errors are: erratic toss; ball not placed high enough, thus losing power and angle; not watching the ball.

Women: Concentrate especially on developing a spin serve rather than a flat one. The motion of throwing is unnatural to most women and subsequently their serves are pushes. Throwing the head of the racket at the ball will increase power and spin. Visualize the ball as a cube and try to lop off the upper right-hand corner.

Men: Avoid swinging so hard at the ball that you drop your head or turn your body square to the net too soon. By dropping your head or turning too early, your power is sapped. Keep the serve a fluid motion and the ball will have plenty of pace.

THE VOLLEY

When you start your volley practice, stand about ten feet from the net waiting for the ball. This encourages you to move forward quickly, meeting the ball well out in front. Practice control as well as power in your volleys. Depth and control are essential on any volley that is not an outright winner. Stand to the left or right of the center line, alternating hitting forehand and backhand volleys deep to the opposite corner. Your opponent will know their direction and be able to supply you with a steady flow. When you've gained a certain proficiency with the volley, a challenging and extremely beneficial drill positions you on the service line opposite your opponent exchanging continuous volleys back and forth. Common errors are too big a swing, loose wrist, and meeting the ball too late.

Women: The tendency is to flap at the ball rather than punching through it. Use a neutral chopper grip and keep the wrist firm throughout.

Men: Most men like the action at the net but fail to watch the ball closely and take an over-zealous swipe.

Control your swing, concentrate on anticipating the path, and intercept the ball well out in front.

THE LOB AND OVERHEAD

This is the ideal and seldom-used practice duo. Select an opponent to alternate hitting lobs and smashes with you. When you lob, concentrate on keeping the stroke solid. Don't flick at the ball with a loose wrist; this results in erratic lobbing. Practice height and depth while aiming for the backhand side of your opponent. This is also good running practice as you're required to chase down the opponent's smashes. In practicing the overhead don't be too ambitious at first. Keep in mind the need to contact the ball firmly, aiming for different spots in the court. Practice getting off the mark quickly with short skip steps to position yourself under the ball.

Men and Women: Don't neglect this drill. Our guess is you're not practicing these shots enough; ninety-nine percent mixed doubles teams are woefully weak in these two areas. Becoming proficient in the overhead and lob will put you in a class by yourself and make you the envy of your mixed doubles opponents. Overhead and lob practice is a good workout and any improvement is invaluable. Above all, devote full attention to your practice as well as your play. Your mind controls the moves. Wish as you might, they just aren't instinctive. Good shots, proper habits, and intelligent playmaking are dependent on your concentration. If we were asked to name one aspect of tennis that is the biggest weakness of players of all levels, it would be a lack of concentration. You must shut everything out of your mind except the job at hand. Concentration, like your backhand, needs to be practiced and developed. Applying yourself whenever you step on the court for practice or play is the best and most rewarding way to better tennis.

CAROLE: *In 1964, Clark and I were playing in the first national husband-and-wife competition at Forest Hills. An early round match had us playing on one of the numerous courts that seem to stretch as far as the eye can see. There were players all around us, and the distractions were numerous. We were having our difficulties, to say the least. Clark seemed to be in another world. Finally my patience gave out: "Darn it Clark, you're not concentrating!" His reply was immediate, direct, and most informative regarding his concentration lapse: "Oh, yes, I am concentrating—on the girl three courts down." My reaction is unprintable but Clark's concentration improved in a great hurry, indeed. Drastic measures are sometimes called for in such circumstances.*

CHAPTER 7

Equipment and Clothing

Rackets and stringing are a never-ending source of discussion and varied opinion for most players. There are literally hundreds of different combinations, each with its own value and limitation. The advent of metal rackets caused a raging controversy over metal's effectiveness versus the traditional wood. The cries of "better response," "worse response," "too stiff," "too whippy," "too heavy," "too light," abound. Some models have tried to incorporate the best aspects of both. The truth is, as long as there's a market, there will always be "new and better" models. The differences between the metal and wood, however, are quite simple. The metal rackets are generally stiffer and quicker flexing, and most models have a circular face. Because the metal racket offers less wind resistance, it cuts a smoother path through the air and can be whipped with greater ease than wood. The metal does impart more speed and pace to the ball, but the subsequent loss of control due to the smaller "sweet spot" (center of strings where the ball strikes), and shortened time the ball stays on the strings, is sometimes a disadvantage. A ball hit off center is more likely to go awry with a metal racket. You must weigh the advantanges of speed with metal versus the greater control of wood. Although we both use metal rackets now, we started with wood. So our advice to beginners or learning players is to start with a wooden racket. Later on, when your strokes are more grooved and your game has taken on certain patterns, switch to metal if you feel the need for more power. There are advantages and disadvantages to both but neither is a "cure-all" or an adequate excuse when your shots fail. The individual swinging the racket makes the difference.

CAROLE: *I have friends who have experimented with almost every type of racket on the market. Their game may improve for a while with one type, but then they develop another ill and change again. It's a vicious circle and an expensive one to boot.*

Whether you prefer wood or metal, however, take care to choose a racket that suits your physique. It should be heavy enough to give you desired power as well as light enough to wield quickly and easily. The rapid pace of modern tennis requires that you be completely in control of the racket, so guard against selecting a racket that controls you. Grip size and weight are personal matters. Choose a racket that feels the best in *your* hand. It's a good rule to sample all sizes. Using your regular "shake hands" grip, test swing several until you find one that suits you. Remember, for an unstrung racket you must attach a swing weight to duplicate the feel of a strung racket. The grip sizes go from four and a half to five, and weights from light to medium to heavy. Women will generally feel more comfortable with a lighter, smaller-grip racket, but men shouldn't be swayed into picking a heavy model out of male pride. There are very few players, indeed, strong enough to swing the heavy models. Medium-weight models with slight variations in balance should provide all the power any man needs.

Stringing involves several considerations: material, tightness, and cost. Synthetic nylon strings are a long-lasting and economical choice. Strung at between fifty-two- and fifty-eight-pound tension, nylon is effective for most casual or weekend players. On the other hand, natural "gut" provides the serious player with more responsive stringing. It can be strung effectively at higher tension without losing its resiliency. But the cost goes up along with quality—twice as much for the higher grades. Natural gut is also adversely affected by dampness and is more likely to break or wear out than nylon. Good players pamper their rackets. Treat yours with care. If you've spent forty dollars on the frame and twenty dollars on stringing, don't leave it in damp places, or chuck it around like an old shoe. When not in use, it should be kept in a cover, and press if wood. Excessive heat or moisture will shorten the life of strings and frame, so be careful where you store the racket.

Grips usually wear out before frames, but they're inexpensive and easily changed. Surprisingly, most players will tolerate an old or faulty grip to the detriment of their game. When the grip gets worn down, smooth, or loses its "tackiness," have your local retailer put on a new one, or do it yourself. It's an easy process, and if you have a spare one along, it can be done in five minutes on the spot. Choose the material that feels the best to you—leather (genuine or synthetic) with varying degrees of roughness—and then change it whenever it loses the right feel. Having a good grip on the racket is essential for confident shot-making.

When selecting tennis balls, you usually get what you pay for. Cheap balls don't last very long. They lose their bounce and cover sooner than quality balls. Any leading brand of top-grade balls will give you more enjoyment and last longer. The cost is reasonable and the product is USLTA approved. There are dozens of different kinds on the market: clay-court balls, grass-court balls, hard-court, heavy-duty balls, all-purpose balls, and bright-colored balls for indoors. Choose those that are best suited for the surface you're playing on. When they've lost their zip and bounce, throw them in a bucket and save them for your private serving practice.

CLOTHING

In our fashion-conscious world, even tennis has a myriad of functional and attractive tennis outfits for men and women. But comfort should not be sacrificed for fashion. Make sure your shorts or dresses are practical and don't restrict your movements. The new fabrics—double knits and synthetics, et cetera—have made more styles available. There are new imaginative outfits to be seen every year. The controversy over white versus colored tennis wear has received notable attention in recent years. Tradition is going by the wayside as more and more professionals opt for colored shirts and color-coordinated outfits. The USLTA now allows pastel combinations, and pressure is being exerted for an even more relaxed clothing code. The traditional "white is right" adage does have its pluses, however. On those scorching summer days, white reflects the sun, rather than absorb it as a darker color will. It's a functional color, always looks well, and doesn't show perspiration. Whatever your choice, however, an effort should be made to keep your tennis clothing bright and clean, at least before the match. You'll feel better in neat attire and probably will play better, too.

Proper tennis shoes are an absolute necessity. Lightweight canvas or synthetic uppers with a patterned sole are good for all surfaces. On asphalt or hard courts, a heavier-duty sole is advisable for cushioning effect and longer wear. On clay or grass, a lighter, thinner-soled model may be used. In any case, the shoe should fit snugly to prevent the foot from moving about inside—the main cause of blisters. Wearing two pairs of socks insures a good fit and greater cushioning effect. Remember, good footwork is an important part of tennis; you don't want to be hindered by ill-chosen or inappropriate footwear.

CHAPTER 8

Staging Your Own Mixed Doubles Tourney

Perhaps you'd like to have your own weekend mixed doubles tournament. Probably there are a couple of real "aces" in your group, a couple of real clunkers or novices, and a group of average players. How best to combine the whole bunch to provide the most enjoyment for everyone? You'd like to challenge both expert and novice alike, without insulting the beginner or handicapping the better player. It can be done, and with lots of tennis for everyone.

A straight elimination tournament just won't do; half the group would be out of it after only one match. So have a series of eliminations and consolations. First of all, you have to select the teams. The only restriction to make is that husband and wife may not play together, nor may the best man and woman play together. Beyond that, partners may choose as they wish. If there are strangers in the group or decisions can't be reached on partners, then the old "draw from the hat" is the fastest and fairest method. You'd be surprised the number of delightful combinations that arise from this method.

CAROLE: *Early in my career, I was the tennis hostess at the Beverly Hills Hotel. Every year the hotel spon-*

sored a celebrity mixed doubles tournament for charity. On one such occasion, the tournament committee decided I should be the "man" and play with Katherine Hepburn. The laughter was raucous at this all-woman "mixed doubles" team. But we had the last laugh and won the tournament. You shouldn't have to go to this extreme, though.

Let's imagine you have sixteen teams. There are no seedings so every team plays a first-round match. For expediency's sake, the first match will be a "pro" set, i.e., the first team to reach eight games wins the set. If the teams reach seven-all, there will be a sudden-death five-out-of-nine-point tie breaker to determine the winner.*

First round winners advance to the second round and the losers go to a consolation round of the losing eight teams. Let's examine a chart to make this clearer. For the purposes of identification we'll call the teams by color. The winners' bracket is to the right. The consolation bracket is to the left.

The second round of both the winners' and the consolation bracket is again a "pro" set with tie breaker at seven-all. The winners of the second round in the winners' bracket (to the right) advance to the third

---

*The tie breaker is played as follows: The first team to win five points wins the set. The regular order of serving is maintained. At seven-all the player on team A due to serve, serves two points. The server from team B then serves two points without switching sides. The teams then change sides and team A partner serves twice. If the match is still undecided, team B partner serves the remaining three points. If the match reaches four-all, the receiving team has the option of selecting the court to which the final serve will be made.

round as do the winners in the second round of the consolation bracket (to the left). At this juncture, the losers of second-round matches in both brackets drop down to a second consolation of two brackets. In effect you have eight semi-final matches and every team is scheduled to play their third match. The losers are playing losers and the winners are playing winners with the result that most matches should by now be fairly well matched. For this round we recommend two out of three sets for all matches with a tie breaker at six–all in any set. The winners of the semifinal matches make up four sets of finals involving the eight remaining teams. The other eight teams may start a third consolation along the same pattern, or bide their time until another day. After all, we have contrived to get eight finalists from a field of sixteen teams. It's sad but true that everyone can't be a winner. Every team has had at least three good matches and the finalists will have had four. This provides plenty of tennis for all, and no one's ego or desire to play has been slighted. There's ample opportunity to show your stuff and win a match or two.

We advise that in a weekend tournament, three rounds be played on Saturday and the four finals be scheduled for Sunday. The eliminated teams provide an audience for the finals or they may wish to take the casual opportunity to play one of the other losing teams.

A word to the wise: Organizing sixteen teams to play this many matches is not always an easy proposition, especially if court space is limited. It helps to be prompt for matches and courteous to the tournament

Winners →

red
white   } white
                        } white
gold   } *gold
yellow
                                    } pink
black   } *green
green
                        } pink
brown   } pink
pink
                                                } ?
orange   } *maroon
maroon
                        } blue
grey   } blue
blue
                                    } blue
beige   } beige
fuschia
                        } beige
purple   } *crimson
crimson

*These four teams go to a second consolation winners bracket (page 96)

← <u>First Consolation</u>

<u>red</u>

<u>red</u>

<u>yellow</u>*

<u>red</u>

<u>black</u>*

<u>brown</u>

<u>brown</u>

<u>?</u>

<u>orange</u>

<u>orange</u>

<u>grey</u>*

<u>purple</u>

<u>fuschia</u>*

<u>purple</u>

<u>purple</u>

*These four teams go to a second consolation losers bracket (page 96)

Second Consolation

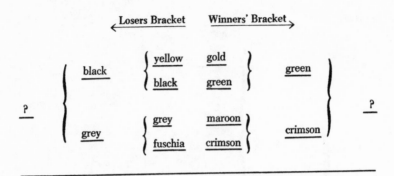

director. He may need a few complimentary words at times to soothe his harried disposition. An enjoyable and challenging tennis tournament of this nature with perhaps an informal Saturday-night gathering for all the teams is an ideal way to spend a weekend.

CHAPTER 9

"It's Not Whether You Win or Lose But..."

So far, we've discussed the more or less direct and functional means of enjoying and winning at mixed doubles. Stroke production, tactics, practice, and concentration are all basics of winning tennis. But there is some frosting you may add to the cake. One-upsmanship or "psyching" can be the final touch that makes your tennis experiences memorable occasions. Psyching is the subtle art of putting your opponent at a mental disadvantage—taking his thunder and turning it into a whimper, putting thoughts in his head he's never considered, pulling his chain, setting him up for unsuspected disasters, caressing his ego to the point of monstrous overconfidence—in general, getting the upperhand, even before the match has begun.

In mixed doubles some very effective pre-match psyching can be applied. The velvet hammer technique is an old standby. The woman might follow the first greeting with such comments as: "Isn't it nice you two are playing together despite all the talk about your inability to team well. We'll try to make it fun for you." Or to the other woman: "Oh, what a cute, dainty racket you have. How do you ever manage to get the ball over the net?" Likewise, the man can casually pick up his opponent's racket and remark: "I understand these heavy sledge-hammer type rackets are terrible for the net game and the best way to get tennis elbow." Even if his racket is completely normal, the seed of doubt will have been planted. Every missed shot will compound his doubts, and he may even baby his serve for fear of the dreaded "tennis elbow." Or, testing his strings, you might add with a concerned look: "Gee, this gut feels pretty mushy—must have been a bad lot, probably a lot of fat in it." He may have no idea what you mean, but he'll think about it.

Sometimes women deal the men the cruelest blow. One of the deadliest jibes always concerns a man's girth and the condition of his tennis game. The woman can casually remark to her male opponent while eyeing his stomach: "Too bad you've played so little this year; I bet you miss the exercise and no one likes to play mediocre tennis." Even if he's been playing every day all summer that one will stick in his craw. Careful though; this type of remark has been known to backfire. He may become a veritable Rod Laver just to spite you.

Once on the court, many a good team has been beaten by weaker opponents through adept "psyching." Never let on that your opponents may be better than you are. If the early going seems to favor them, wait for a moment when you've hit one of your best shots by them, then casually remark to your partner for all to hear: "I always take time to warm up—makes it more interesting." Any exchanges that seem to patronize their play are always to your benefit: "Good try," or "Sorry, a bit long," after shots they've missed. If you spot a weakness in an opponent, make sure he realizes you know about it. A stage whisper to your partner is best: "Can't hit a backhand to save his life, can he?" They're sure to over-compensate or tighten up under that thrust. Always compliment opponents on their lucky shots as if they were planned. Make them think tough shots are easy, and then when you really need a point, hit that lob to the backhand they've been lucking out on. Nine times out of ten, they'll miss the shot, having gotten careless and overconfident.

CLARK: *In an early round match at Longwood one year, Marty Riessen and I were in danger of losing to an unheralded team whose names we didn't even know. As a matter of fact, our opponents were about to serve for the match in the final set, as we changed sides. Things were very grave indeed! Passing our opponents in the change I casually mentioned: "You know, you guys will have beaten the National Clay Court doubles champions if you win the next game." That did it; our opponents choked completely, lost their serve, the set, and the match. Just a passing remark, but a rapier-like one at that!*

In a close match when both teams are gritting for every point and the concentration on both sides is fierce, gaze sleepily at the sky and casually remark: "What a great day just to be outdoors; this is the best relaxation I know." While you say this, however, be thinking exactly what you'll do with the next shot or how you plan to attack their service. Your opponents will be nonplussed at your apparent composure. You've not only overcome your tightness but perhaps destroyed their concentration with such an extra-ordinary remark under pressure. On the surface you're cool as a cucumber; underneath you're fighting harder than ever. On those close shots that your opponents miss by only inches, nonchalance is the best profile to take. Treat the shot as if it were five feet out. Casually walk away from it remarking in your best matter-of-fact tone: "You're long, bad luck." Hide your sigh of relief and feign an air of indifference. Your opponents will be muttering to themselves while you're preparing for the next exchange.

Much of the fun and satisfaction in psyching is on-the-spot inprovisation. Let your imagination react to the special circumstances at hand. Above all keep a smile on your face and an air of innocence in your remarks. A classic example comes to mind: In the 1971 Wimbledon final, Stan Smith was ahead two sets to one against John Newcombe, serving in the fourth set. His first major crown seemed to be in his pocket, as John was struggling badly and having little luck against Stan's power. Newcombe, coming to net for a short volley, slipped and fell heavily at the service line. He lay motionless; the crowd was deathly quiet; Stan peered over the net with some apprehension: "You O.K., John?" No reply as the silence continued. Finally, Newcombe struggled to his feet and pantomimed a grotesquely broken arm with a huge grin on his face. The crowd roared and Stan was completely bemused. His concentration and momentum destroyed, Smith lost his service, the next two sets, and the championship. Newcombe had literally stolen the crown from him with a master "psyche" job.

ETIQUETTE OF THE GAME

The rules of tennis are explicit and basically common-sense rulings. The game itself is not complex nor are the rules. But like any sport, tennis has areas in which controversy may arise. If these areas are not specifically covered in the rules, it is because they are deemed best left up to the better judgment of the player—in other words, an unwritten code of "etiquette" for the game. Any game, sport, or activity can be ruined by the dud who insists on behaving in an impolite or inconsiderate fashion. Tennis is no exception. Here are some tennis misdemeanors that every player ought to guard against.

1. In mixed doubles squabbling or bickering with your partner in an unhappy alliance is strictly taboo. Whatever your troubles as a team, your effectiveness will only deteriorate under duress of open criticism. Your opponents will be embarrassed for you, and all enjoyment is quickly drained from the game. Likewise, displays of temper are extremely unseemly. No one can blame you for an occasional anguished exclamation, but tantrums that often follow bad luck or poor play are just childish. Throwing your racket or zinging a ball around the court after a bad shot are not only poor manners but destructive. Why pay forty dollars for a racket and then slam it on the ground? Recently, we saw a man (who should have known better) belt a ball across the net in frustration after netting an easy volley, only to see it strike his opponent in the back of the head. Very painful to the opponent but far more embarrassing for the poor fool who let his temper run away with him. In mixed doubles when the friendly and social aspects of the game are at a premium, temper displays are downright ridiculous—the height of impoliteness.

2. There is at one time or another in most matches a

controversy over a close line call. The proper procedure here is quite simple: If you have not seen the ball clearly as out, you are obliged to play it as good. Make your "out" calls or "let" calls with no delay. Don't wait until the ball has crossed the net three or four times and then decide the serve was long. Either call it immediately or don't call it at all. Nor should you solicit the opinion of an innocent onlooker. Giving your opponent the benefit of the doubt avoids juvenile controversy that is a detriment to the game. By the same token there are those who insist on calling balls that are close but in, "good." This is most disconcerting to an opponent who has hit an effective shot only to be distracted by a loud affirmation of such from the other end of the court. All players are obliged to continue play until an "out" call has been made. An unnecessary "good" call only confuses matters.

3. Before each point, the serving team should give the score. This eliminates any doubt and avoids controversy during long games when a series of hard-fought points may confuse all four players.

4. The use of delaying or distracting tactics is just plain bad manners. Taking excessive time to change courts or dawdling between points slows the natural and pleasant pace of tennis. After all, the rules state that play shall be continuous. Distractions such as waving your arms while your opponent serves or dropping your racket just before he serves are bush tactics. Talking during a point other than team commands such as "yours" or "drop it" is also most distracting. Any intentional, malicious attempt to disrupt play should be avoided.

5. Most importantly, play with all the verve and determination you can muster. Never concede a point, game, or set until the last shot. You will respect yourself, your partner will appreciate the effort, and your opponents will admire you. If you should lose, however, don't begrudge your opponents the congratulations they deserve. They want the satisfaction of feeling they've won fair and square.

If you win (and winning is more fun no matter how you slice it); be worthy of the victory. Be gracious and compliment your opponents where they deserve it. One of the best winning lines in tennis is: "That was fun; let's do it again."

Yours for better tennis

The world at large has a tendency to look at professional and world class tennis players with a somewhat envious eye. Somehow we seem to be above the day-to-day struggles that ordinary tennis players have with their game. Our ability, like that of a high-wire performer, is seen as a special gift—one that puts us in the sporting limelight shared by only a select few. Nothing could be farther from the truth. "If we could only play tennis like the Graebners..." is a very human reaction for the average player to have. We're flattered and honored. But we admit candidly that we consider ourselves to have been supremely fortunate in our careers. Please have no delusions about our seemingly invincible gifts on the tennis court. For every moment of struggle you have had on the court, for all the frustrations with your game, we have had our own and many more. The answer is that the pursuit of excellence is an infinitely rewarding experience in any field. Tennis is simply a *great* game, whether a vocation or a recreation, and aspiring to be better at it is honest tribute to its worth. Our lifetime connection with the sport has given us the lucky opportunity to share *our* tennis with you. We hope *your* tennis is better for it.

Clark and Carole Graebner

ABOUT THE AUTHORS

Clark started playing tennis under his father's tute-
lage and took up the game seriously at the age of ten.
From being both singles and doubles champion in the
boys' division he went on to be graduated from
Northwestern University, and then to garner trophies
in major tournaments all over the world. Three times a
Davis Cup singles player, winner of the National
singles title on three surfaces, he is currently ranked
in the top ten in the United States for the seventh
time.

Carole is a product of the public courts of California,
chiefly in Santa Monica where she grew up and was
judiciously coached in winning ways by her grandfather. A finalist in 1964 at Forest Hills, and ranked
No. 1 in the world in doubles (with Nancy Richey) in
1966, she competes infrequently these days, but Wimbledon and Forest Hills still see her in action occasionally. She is Beauty, Tennis, and Fashion Consultant for
Bonne Bell Cosmetics, Inc., and an advertising execu-
tive for *World Tennis* magazine.

It's too early to assess the tennis talents of the
Graebners' six-year-old daughter, Cameron, and her
four-year-old brother, Clark.